# THIS HOLY MYSTERY

## A United Methodist Understanding of Holy Communion

### Gayle Carlton Felton

**DISCIPLESHIP RESOURCES**

PO BOX 340003
NASHVILLE TN
37203-0003
www.discipleshipresources.org

## Committee Members

L. Edward Phillips, Chairperson
Daniel T. Benedict, Jr.
Michael J. Coyner
Jerome King Del Pino
Gayle Carlton Felton
Thelma H. Flores
Barbara Thorington Green
Karen A. Greenwaldt
Susan W. Hassinger
Sally Havens

Dong Hyun (David) Kim
Jon E. McCoy
Sophie Pieh
Arturo L. Razon, Jr.
Bruce W. Robbins
Frank E. Trotter, Jr.
Karen Westerfield Tucker
Hans Vaxby
Josiah U. Young, III

## Notes About This Book:

Scripture quotations, unless otherwise indicated, are from the New Revised Standard Version Bible, copyright 1989, Division of Christian Education of the National Council of the Churches of Christ in the United States of America. Used by permission. All rights reserved.

*BOD*, *Discipline*, and *Book of Discipline* refer to *The Book of Discipline of The United Methodist Church—2004*. Quotations from the *Book of Discipline* are copyright © 2004 by The United Methodist Publishing House. Used by permission.

*BOR* refers to *The Book of Resolutions of The United Methodist Church—2004*. Quotations from the *Book of Resolutions* are copyright © 2004 by The United Methodist Publishing House. Used by permission.

*BOW* refers to *The United Methodist Book of Worship*, copyright © 1992 The United Methodist Publishing House.

*UMH* refers to *The United Methodist Hymnal*, copyright © 1989 The United Methodist Publishing House.

Quotations from John Wesley are from the Jackson edition of *The Works of John Wesley* unless otherwise indicated.

Cover and book design by Nanci H. Lamar

Edited by Linda R. Whited and Cindy S. Harris

ISBN 0-88177-457-X

Library of Congress Control Number 2004114305

# Contents

# Introduction

## To the Leader

This study edition is designed for use in our work of teaching and learning from "This Holy Mystery." It is organized into seven sessions but is flexible enough to be utilized differently and could easily be expanded into twice as many sessions. There is likely to be more material than can be covered, and participants should be encouraged to continue their own study beyond the group sessions. (Each participant should have a copy of this study edition.)

Each session contains four types of material:
- the text of "This Holy Mystery," approved by the 2004 General Conference;
- commentary on the section of text used in that session;
- general suggestions for "Teaching and Learning";
- a section entitled "To Expand the Study" that includes suggestions and resources particularly relevant to clergy and for use in academic settings.

The intention is for the participants to read the text of "This Holy Mystery" and the commentary in this guide before each gathering. You, as leader, will plan how to use the "Teaching and Learning" suggestions first, followed by the suggestions in "To Expand the Study" as supplementary material in groups where those suggestions are appropriate. Read the suggestions and questions in both sections as you prepare to lead the group. Note that there are sometimes suggestions for advance assignments for the group in addition to their reading the document text and commentary for the session. Plan early to take advantage of those opportunities to involve participants in the teaching. (Notice that the suggestions that may require advance preparation by the participants are marked with the symbol *.)

Much fine material on Holy Communion by outstanding scholars has previously been published, and I have made specific recommendations to facilitate finding and utilizing those resources, which are integral to the study. First, though, you should become thoroughly familiar with the interpretive document (printed in the wider, inside columns) and with the Services of Word and Table in *The United Methodist Hymnal* or in *The United Methodist Book of Worship*. (Services I and V are included in the Appendix of this study guide.)

As you plan to lead a group in study, always look ahead to see what materials you will need for each session and what assignments or other plans need to be made for the next session.

As you teach, avoid simply lecturing, even though a lot of material needs

In 1996 the General Conference of The United Methodist Church approved "By Water and the Spirit: A United Methodist Understanding of Baptism" as an official interpretive document for the church. Since then many groups have used this resource in teaching our people clearer comprehension and increased appreciation for the sacrament of baptism. Soon there were queries about the possibility of a similar document addressing the church's other sacrament, Holy Communion. A survey conducted by the General Board of Discipleship confirmed that United Methodists want such a resource.

Following authorization by the 2000 General Conference, a study committee of nineteen members worked during the next quadrennium to develop an interpretive document for Holy Communion. The committee was a diverse group of laypeople and clergy, including bishops, general agency secretaries, seminary professors, deacons, and elders. There were six meetings, each for three to four days, and much communication between the meetings. Meetings were held in all five jurisdictions of the church in the United States. These sessions included interaction with representative people in each area. Similar "listening posts" were held in central conferences in Africa, Northern and Central Europe, and the Philippines. After each meeting of the committee, a draft of the document was written to serve as both a record and a source of the ongoing process. The study committee shared these drafts

with the church by posting them on the General Board of Discipleship website and seeking responses. Much correspondence was generated and used in continuation of the work.

"This Holy Mystery: A United Methodist Understanding of Holy Communion" was overwhelmingly approved by the 2004 General Conference. For the first time in our history, the denomination has an official, comprehensive statement of the practice and theology of the Lord's Supper.

The General Conference also called for the implementation and wide use of this interpretive document. This commentary and study guide represents a part of the effort to respond to that directive and to encourage Christian conferencing at all levels of the church, with the aim of "a richer sacramental life" for United Methodists.

—Gayle Carlton Felton

to be conveyed. Be sure that each participant has a copy of this study guide, and encourage each person to record questions and make notes in it. Without making anyone uncomfortable, encourage every member of the group to participate in discussion.

## Other Resources You Will Need

### United Methodist Resources

(When these resources are used in the commentary, page numbers for the location of the material will be identified as needed using these acronyms.)
- *The Book of Discipline—2004* (BOD)
- *The Book of Resolutions—2004* (BOR)
- *The Book of Worship* (BOW)
- *The United Methodist Hymnal* (UMH)
- *The Faith We Sing* (TFWS)
- *By Water and the Spirit* (the study guide published by Discipleship Resources or the document in *The Book of Resolutions*) (BWTS)

### Other Print Resources

- *American Methodist Worship*, by Karen B. Westerfield Tucker (Oxford University Press, 2001).
- "Baptism, Eucharist and Ministry" (World Council of Churches, 1982).
- *Creative Preaching on the Sacraments*, by Craig A. Satterlee and Lester Ruth (Discipleship Resources, 2001).
- *Eucharist and Eschatology*, by Geoffrey Wainwright (Oxford, 1981).
- *Eucharist: Christ's Feast With the Church*, by Laurence Hull Stookey (Abingdon Press, 1993).
- *The Meaning of Holy Communion in The United Methodist Church*, by E. Byron Anderson (Discipleship Resources, 2000; updated 2005).
- *Quarterly Review*, Winter 1999–2000, Fall 2002 (General Board of Higher Education and Ministry of The United Methodist Church). For free downloads of *Quarterly Review* articles used in this study guide, go to www.discipleshipresources.org/images/drdownloads/holy_mystery.asp.
- *Sacraments and Discipleship: Understanding Baptism and the Lord's Supper in a United Methodist Context*, by Mark W. Stamm, O.S.L. (Discipleship Resources, 2001).
- *Sacraments as God's Self-Giving: Sacramental Practice and Faith*, by James F. White (Abingdon, 1983).
- *The Sacraments in Protestant Practice and Faith*, by James F. White (Abingdon Press, 1999).
- *Sunday Dinner: The Lord's Supper and the Christian Life*, by William H. Willimon (The Upper Room, 1981).
- *Worship Matters: A United Methodist Guide to Ways to Worship, Volume 1*, E. Byron Anderson, editor (Discipleship Resources, 1999).

### Materials

- Current articles or news stories related to Holy Communion
- Bibles
- markerboard or newsprint and markers
- piano and pianist

# This Holy Mystery: A United Methodist Understanding of Holy Communion

## Part One: There Is More to the Mystery

The story is told of a little girl whose parents had taken her forward to receive Holy Communion. Disappointed with the small piece of bread she was given to dip in the cup, the child cried loudly, "I want more! I want more!" While embarrassing to her parents and amusing to the pastor and congregation, this little girl's cry accurately expresses the feelings of many contemporary United Methodist people. We want more! We want more than we are receiving from the sacrament of Holy Communion as it is practiced in our churches.

According to the results of a survey conducted by the General Board of Discipleship prior to the 2000 General Conference, there is a strong sense of the importance of Holy Communion in the life of individual Christians and of the church. Unfortunately, there is at least an equally strong sense of the absence of any meaningful understanding of Eucharistic theology and practice. United Methodists recognize that grace and spiritual power are available to them in the sacrament, but too often they do not feel enabled to receive these gifts and apply them in their lives. Many laypeople complain of sloppy practice, questionable theology, and lack of teaching and guidance. Both clergy and laity recognize the crucial need for better education of pastors in sacramental theology and practice. The concern for improved education is coupled with a call for accountability. Bishops, district superintendents,

The goal of this study is the renewal of worship in United Methodist congregations through enhanced appreciation of the sacrament of Holy Communion. Unfortunately, many of our churches have strayed far away from the rich liturgical and sacramental heritage of Christian tradition. Our continuing declines in membership and worship attendance are indicators, warnings even, that our worship life is in crucial need of revitalization. It is not just that we desire larger numbers of people. It is that we need to provide deepened experiences of encounter with God through our worship to as many people as possible.

"By Water and the Spirit: A United Methodist Understanding of Baptism" has elevated and expanded our understanding of Holy Baptism as the source of our identity and mission as Christians. Its provisions have been incorporated into *The Book of Discipline* to clarify the relationship between baptism and church membership and the role of the sacrament in the lifelong journey of faith. "This Holy Mystery: A United Methodist Understanding of Holy Communion" has similar purpose. We believe that study of this document will yield increased appreciation for the centrality of the sacrament in the worship experience and enable United Methodist people to draw nourishment and strength for their ongoing journeys of faith.

In recent times, Holy Communion has been the focus of some high-profile debates

both within and between various parts of the Christian community. The Roman Catholic Church occasioned controversy when some of its bishops threatened to deny the sacrament to politicians, including the 2004 Democratic presidential candidate, who did not oppose abortion rights. In a few cases, bishops have refused to recognize as valid the first Communion of children when a non-wheat wafer was used (due to celiac sprue disease or severe allergies). Denominations are changing their practices to accommodate changed circumstances. Some Assemblies of God churches now serve Communion at their Sunday evening services because the morning services are so crowded that Communion then is unwieldy. In some congregations, including many Southern Baptist ones, pre-packaged units of a wafer and a small plastic cup of grape juice are passed up and down the pews on cardboard trays. Presbyterians are increasingly receiving the elements at the rail rather than in the pews. Some of their congregations now use wine rather than grape juice and prefer the mode of intinction. Presbyterians and Lutherans are among those joining United Methodism in encouraging weekly celebration of the Lord's Supper. While the liturgies and practices of the mainline denominations have increased in similarity, both among themselves and with Roman Catholicism, the practices of other Christian groups—many of them rapidly growing—are diversifying in response to changing societal expectations and cultural conditions.[1]

The results of the General Board of Discipleship survey of interests and concerns related to Holy Communion are both encouraging and disturbing. They indicate that United Methodists want meaningful celebrations of the sacrament and realize that Holy Communion offers something vital to

and other annual conference and general church authorities are urged to prepare their pastors better and to hold them accountable for their sacramental theology, practice, and teaching. Many of the people surveyed are plainly resentful of the lack of leadership they believe they are receiving in these areas. These results are troubling and must provoke the church to reexamination and recommitment.

These results are also exciting and challenging! They reveal a deep hunger for the riches of divine grace made available to us through Holy Communion, for real communion with Jesus Christ and with Christian people. They show that United Methodists want our faith to be enlivened and made more relevant to our daily lives. How can our church best respond to the wonderful hunger of its people for "this holy mystery"[1] (*BOW*; page 39)?

United Methodists share with many other Christians an increased interest in the study and celebration of the sacraments. For the last several decades we have been actively seeking to recover and revitalize appreciation of Holy Baptism and Holy Communion. Our current services of the Baptismal Covenant and Word and Table are the fruit of a long process of development that began in the 1960's and culminated in their adoption by the 1984 General Conference and publication in *The United Methodist Hymnal* approved in 1988. The change in location of these sacramental rituals from the back to the front of the *Hymnal* is an intentional expression of their significance in the life of the community of faith. In 1996, the General Conference approved "By Water and the Spirit: A United Methodist Understanding of Baptism" as an official interpretive and teaching document for the church. "This Holy Mystery: A United Methodist Understanding of Holy Communion" is submitted to the 2004 General Conference with the same purpose. Both of these documents reflect United Methodism's efforts to reclaim its sacramental heritage and to be in accord with ecumenical movements in sacramental theology and practice.

*This Holy Mystery* is characterized by the effort to avoid rigidity on the one hand and indifference on the other. Neither extreme is true to our heritage nor faithful to the Spirit who leads the church forward in the work of making disciples living toward the new creation. The document is made up of two main parts. The expository introduction titled "Part One: There Is More to the Mystery" describes the document's development and provides grounding in historical tradition and sacramental theology. "Part Two: Christ Is Here: Experiencing the Mystery" is organized by principles. Under each principle, "Background" provides an explanation for the principle, while "Practice" provides guidelines for applying the principle. The principles make assertions that are truthful and doctrinally clear. They honor the historic and ecumenical center of the Christian church's theology and practice. The committee has endeavored to explain in the "Background" sections how the principles are rooted in the theology and practice of Christians past and present, particularly United Methodist Christians. In the "Practice" sections we have applied the principles to contemporary sacramental practices of the church in the various contexts of United Methodism.

The church is always universal and particular, catholic and local, united and diverse. United Methodists vary geographically, racially, and culturally. *This Holy Mystery* invites United Methodists to share common understandings while allowing for appropriate, faithful applications. Some United Methodist practices differ from those of other Christian traditions. Being truthful about these differences recognizes our ties and responsibility to the wider church while claiming God's work in leading us to affirm distinctive understandings and practices. Both within our own United Methodist community and in fellowship with other traditions, we reject cavalier or arrogant attitudes. We seek to strengthen the bond of unity by "speaking the truth in love" (Ephesians 4:15) as, with humility and openness, we acknowledge our principles, explain our backgrounds, and affirm our practices.

## Names of the Sacrament

Several terms naming the sacrament are used in past and present Christianity. In *This Holy Mystery* some are used more than others, but all are largely synonymous. *The Lord's Supper* reminds us that Jesus Christ is the host and that we participate at Christ's invitation. This title suggests the eating of a meal, sometimes called the Holy Meal, and makes us think of the meals that Jesus ate with various people both before his death and after his resurrection. The term *the Last Supper* is not appropriately used for the sacrament, but it does encourage us to remember the supper that Jesus ate with his disciples on the night when he was arrested. This emphasis is especially meaningful around Maundy Thursday. The early church appears to have referred to their celebrations as breaking bread (Acts 2:42).

The term *Holy Communion* invites us to focus on the self-giving of the Holy God, which makes the sacrament an occasion of grace, and on

their spiritual lives. The results also make clear that they are dissatisfied with what they are experiencing in their local congregations and even in worship settings on the district and annual conference levels. Our people are asking why. Why is something that is so important often handled so poorly? Why do so many of our pastors not seem to recognize the significance of the sacrament? Why are our Eucharistic services often so abbreviated, so rushed, even trivialized? Why do district superintendents and bishops not ensure that our pastors are well trained in sacramental celebration and hold them accountable for their practices? Here is an obvious challenge to the church as well as a rich opportunity!

The most direct scriptural basis for our observance of the Lord's Supper is found in the New Testament accounts of its institution by Christ. The Gospels of Matthew (26:26-29), Mark (14:22-25), and Luke (22:14-23) contain similar descriptions of the actions and words of Jesus during his meal with the disciples just before he was arrested and crucified. All of these passages include the four-fold pattern that we continue: take, bless, break, and give. All of them record that Jesus called the bread his body and the cup his blood. The ritual is associated by Jesus with the establishment of a covenant between him and his followers. In Luke and in the account in 1 Corinthians 11:23-26, Jesus tells his disciples, "Do this in remembrance of me." John's Gospel has no explicit account of the institution of Holy Communion, but in the sixth chapter there is extended consideration of Christ as the bread of heaven. Eating of Christ's body and drinking his blood is said to be the source of spiritual life.

Holy Communion is practiced by almost all Christian denominations, but with differing understandings. Frequently

these differences are the result of over-emphasis of one meaning of the sacrament to the point of ignoring other meanings. United Methodist theology and practice have their root in the views of our founder, John Wesley, and are influenced significantly by the history of our predecessor denominations in the United States. Wesley's sacramental theology was derived from that of the Church of England, in which he was, and remained, a priest. An amalgam of the teachings of sixteenth-century reformers Martin Luther, John Calvin, and Ulrich Zwingli formed the basis of Anglican understanding. Wesley was also influenced by his study of the early Christian church and of the tradition of Eastern Orthodoxy. Wesley was disappointed by the infrequency and ineffectiveness of the Eucharist as it was offered in the parish churches of his time. He wanted people to have greater access to the sacrament and to apprehend the spiritual power available through it. The Wesleyan movement was a Eucharistic revival as well as an evangelical one.

## Teaching and Learning

### Resources and Materials

- Current articles or news stories related to Holy Communion
- *Quarterly Review*, Fall 2002
- Copies of this book
- *By Water and the Spirit*
- Markerboard or newsprint and markers
- Bibles
- Copies of *The United Methodist Hymnal* and *The Faith We Sing*
- Piano and pianist
- *Eucharist: Christ's Feast With the Church*, by Laurence Hull Stookey
- *The Sacraments in Protestant Practice and Faith*, by James F. White

the holiness of our communion with God and one another. *Eucharist*, from the Greek word for thanksgiving, reminds us that the sacrament is thanksgiving to God for the gifts of creation and salvation. The term *Mass*, used by the Roman Catholic Church, derives from the Latin word *missio*, literally "sending forth," and indicates that this celebration brings the worship service to a close by sending forth the congregation with God's blessing to live as God's people in the world. *The Divine Liturgy* is a name used mostly by churches in the tradition of Eastern Orthodoxy. All of these names refer to the same practice: the eating and drinking of consecrated bread and wine in the worshiping community.

## Background

As early as the Emmaus experience on the day of Resurrection, recorded in Luke 24:13-35, Christians recognized the presence of Jesus Christ in the breaking of bread. The traditional Jewish practice of taking bread, blessing and thanking God, and breaking and sharing the bread took on new meaning for them. When followers of Christ gathered in Jesus' name, the breaking of bread and sharing of the cup was a means of remembering his life, death, and resurrection and of encountering the living Christ. They experienced afresh the presence of their risen Lord and received sustenance for their lives as disciples. As the church organized itself, this custom of Eucharist became the characteristic ritual of the community and the central act of its worship.

Over the centuries, various understandings and practices of Holy Communion have developed. Roman Catholicism teaches that the substance of bread and wine are changed (although not visibly) into the actual body and blood of Christ (sometimes called transubstantiation). Protestant Reformers in the sixteenth century rejected this teaching but had diverse ideas among themselves. Lutherans maintain that Christ's body and blood are truly present in and with the elements of bread and wine in the celebration (sometimes erroneously called corporeal presence or consubstantiation). Ulrich Zwingli, a Swiss reformer, taught that the Lord's Supper is a memorial or reminder of Christ's sacrifice, an affirmation of faith, and a sign of Christian fellowship. Although his name may be unfamiliar, Zwingli's views are widely shared today, especially within evangelical churches. Denominations in the Reformed tradition, following John Calvin, maintain that although Christ's body is in heaven, when Holy Communion is received with true faith, the power of the Holy Spirit nourishes those who partake. The Church of

England affirmed a somewhat similar view in its Catechism and Articles of Religion. These understandings (stated here very simplistically) suggest the range of ideas that were available to John and Charles Wesley and the early Methodists.

## United Methodist Heritage

### Early Methodism

The Methodist movement in eighteenth-century England was an evangelical movement that included a revival of emphasis on the sacraments. The Wesleys recognized the power of God available in the Lord's Supper and urged their followers to draw on that power by frequent participation. The grace available in and through the sacrament was active in conviction, repentance and conversion, forgiveness, and sanctification. John Wesley described the Lord's Supper as "the grand channel whereby the grace of his Spirit was conveyed to the souls of all the children of God."[2] During the years in which Methodism was beginning and growing, Wesley himself communed an average of four to five times a week. His sermon "The Duty of Constant Communion" emphasizes the role of the sacrament in the lives of Christians in ways that are keenly meaningful today. The Wesley brothers wrote and published a collection of 166 *Hymns on the Lord's Supper*, which was used for meditation as well as for singing. The Wesleys understood and taught the multifaceted nature of the Lord's Supper. They wrote about love, grace, sacrifice, forgiveness, the presence of Christ, mystery, healing, nourishment, holiness, and pledge of heaven. They knew that Holy Communion is a powerful means through which divine grace is given to God's people. Our sacramental understandings and practices today are grounded in this heritage.

### Evangelical and United Brethren Roots

The movements that developed into the Church of the United Brethren in Christ and the Evangelical Church began in the late eighteenth century and early nineteenth century in America. From the beginning, relationships between these groups and the Methodists were close and cordial. The beliefs and practices of the three churches were similar. Francis Asbury and Philip William Otterbein were close friends, and Otterbein participated in Asbury's consecration as a Methodist Episcopal bishop. Conversations about possible union began at least as early as 1809 and continued intermittently until the churches finally merged in 1968 to form The United Methodist Church.

*1. "Taste and See: Sacramental Renewal Among United Methodists," by Don E. Saliers, in *Quarterly Review*, Fall 2002 (pages 223–233), offers an insightful introduction to the ideas of this session. If possible, assign sections to members of the group. Ask them to read in advance and be prepared to present ideas in the session.

2. Have as many people who wish to, to answer these questions: What was your most meaningful experience of Holy Communion? Why was it so significant?

3. Examine together the Table of Contents of "This Holy Mystery" (page 3), noting the overall organization of the document and the topics discussed.

4. Discuss: Does the little girl's cry, "I want more," express the feeling of people in your congregation? If so, how can you respond to this desire? If not, how can you engender that desire?

5. Discuss: What is it that we want more of? What changes can you imagine that might make this possible?

6. Read and discuss the brief section on Holy Communion close to the end of *By Water and the Spirit* (in *The Book of Resolutions*, No. 343, page 873–874, or in the study edition of *By Water and the Spirit*, pages 43–44).

7. Discuss: What name(s) for Holy Communion is(are) most commonly used in your congregation? How could your congregation's view of the sacrament be expanded by using other names as well?

8. Read aloud and discuss the passages from the Gospels and 1 Corinthians that are cited on page 9.

9. Read Luke 24:13-34 aloud and talk about how this story helps us to grasp the power

of the Eucharist. Invite the participants to identify the "basic pattern" (*UMH*, page 2) in Luke's telling of the story.

10. Locate the four actions of the ritual—taking, blessing, breaking, and giving, in "A Service of Word and Table I" (beginning on page 6 of *The United Methodist Hymnal* and printed in the Appendix of this study guide). Talk about how they are expressed in words and actions.

11. Tell about your experiences and knowledge of Eucharistic practices in other denominations. What similarities and differences have you observed?

12. Read and discuss the Eucharistic hymns by Charles Wesley in *The United Methodist Hymnal* (Nos. 612–641) and *The Faith We Sing* (Nos. 2254–2269). Compare the other hymns for the Lord's Supper found in the two hymn books to those of Wesley. Sing a few of the Wesley hymns, perhaps as a closing activity.

## To Expand the Study
### (for clergy and in academic settings)

1. Compile and display a list of the main complaints of laypeople about Eucharistic practice as they have experienced it. Allow a brief time for some participants to discuss these complaints, with others sitting nearby to listen and observe.

2. Assess the education and experience that you received before leading your first service of Holy Communion. What further education in the sacraments have you received during your ministry? What kinds of continuing education would enhance your administration of the sacraments?

*3. Ask appropriate people to prepare in advance and present brief summaries of the positions and practices of Roman

Unfortunately, Otterbein and Martin Boehm—founders of the United Brethren—left little written material. The same is true of Evangelical founder Jacob Albright. Therefore, we can make comparatively few references to their theology and practice of Holy Communion. The *Journal* of Christian Newcomer (d. 1830), third United Brethren bishop, records so many occasions of administering and participating in the sacrament that its significance in the life of the church is apparent.

## American Methodism

The early American Methodists, who began arriving in the 1760's, were at first able to receive the sacraments from Anglican churches of which they were considered a part. But the situation soon changed, and Methodists began to reject the English church. As rising tensions between the colonies and England led to the Revolutionary War, most Anglican priests left the country. By the mid 1770's, most Methodists had no access to the sacraments. The missionary preachers sent by John Wesley were laymen, as were the Americans who became preachers. They had no authority to baptize or to offer Holy Communion. Methodists were longing for the sacraments, and it was this need that motivated Wesley to take actions to provide ordained elders for America. In 1784, the Methodist Episcopal Church was created and some preachers were ordained. Still, the number of elders was too small to offer the sacraments regularly to the rapidly increasing number of Methodists. During the decades of the circuit riders, most Methodists were able to receive the Lord's Supper quarterly, at best, when the ordained elder came to their community. The camp meetings of the period were also sacramental occasions where large numbers of people communed. By the late nineteenth century and throughout the twentieth, many Methodist churches were served by ordained elders, but the habit of quarterly Holy Communion remained strong.

American Methodists considered Holy Communion a sacred and solemn event. The tone of the ritual was deeply penitential, calling upon people to repent and having less emphasis on celebration of God's grace. During the nineteenth and twentieth centuries the rich Wesleyan understandings of Eucharist were largely lost, and the sacrament became understood only as a memorial of the death of Christ. In many congregations, attendance on Communion Sunday was low. Revitalization of the Lord's Supper in Methodism, and in the Evangelical and United Brethren churches, started in the mid-twentieth century when the churches began to reclaim their sacramental heritage and create new rituals to express it.

As Methodism spread to other parts of the world, ritual and practice established in America were followed. Over the years, however, there have been certain influences from surrounding Christian traditions. These are to some extent reflected in Holy Communion practice in the central conferences (those beyond the geographic area of the United States).

## Endnotes

1 From "A Service of Word and Table I," © 1972 The Methodist Publishing House; © 1980, 1985, 1989, 1992 UMPH.
2 From "Sermon on the Mount—Discourse Six," III.11.

Catholicism, Eastern Orthodoxy, Lutheranism, Reformed churches, Zwinglianism, and Anglicanism/Episcopalianism. Two valuable sources are *Eucharist: Christ's Feast With the Church*, by Laurence Hull Stookey, Chapter 3, and *The Sacraments in Protestant Practice and Faith*, by James F. White, pages 73–84. Have participants tell about the dominant understandings in their congregations.

*4. Ask participants to read in advance chapters 2, 3, and 4 of Laurence Hull Stookey's *Eucharist: Christ's Feast With the Church* and discuss this material together.

## Endnote

1 Much of this information comes from the article "Churches adjust Communion practices," by Bill Broadway, published in *The Washington Post* and reprinted in *The News & Observer* (Raleigh, North Carolina), September 24, 2004; page 4E.

## Grace and the Means of Grace

Today Holy Communion must be viewed within the larger context of United Methodist theology. In accord with biblical and Christian teaching, we believe that we are sinners, constantly in need of divine grace. We believe that God is gracious and loving, always making available the grace we need. Grace is God's love toward us, God's free and undeserved gift. Several words describe how grace works in our lives. Prevenient grace is that which "comes before" anything we can do to help ourselves. Although we are all bound by our sinful nature, grace gives us enough freedom of will to be able to respond to God. In truth, all grace is prevenient—we cannot move toward God unless God has first moved toward us. God seeks us out, pursues us, calls us to come into the loving relationship that we were created to enjoy. Convicting grace makes us conscious of our sinfulness and urges us to repentance. Justifying grace forgives and puts us into right relationship with God. Sanctifying grace enables us to grow in holiness of life. Perfecting grace molds us into the image of Christ. The grace of God is made available to us through the life, death, and resurrection of Jesus Christ and works in our lives through the presence and power of the Holy Spirit.

While divine grace reaches us any time and in any way that God chooses, God has designated certain means or channels through which grace is most surely and immediately available. John Wesley expressed it this way: "By 'means of grace' I understand outward signs, words, or actions, ordained of God, and appointed for this end, to be the ordinary channels whereby he might convey to men [and women], preventing, justifying, or sanctifying grace."[1]

In the General Rules, Wesley listed these means of grace as "the public worship of God. The ministry of the Word, either read or

Holy Communion must not be seen as an isolated event in the worship life of the church. The sacrament is integral to our experience of how God works in human lives to bring us to salvation. We believe that our relationship with God is broken by our sin and that we are unable to free ourselves from this condition. Our innate human capacities do not enable us to save ourselves; but the God of the Bible, the God made known to us in Jesus Christ, relentlessly seeks us out and woos us back into the relationship that we were created to enjoy. Only because God takes the initiative are we empowered to move toward God. Grace is God's free and unmerited favor, the expression of divine love for us. God acts to enable us to respond to the gift of divine grace. When we do respond, God bestows more grace. As the lifelong process of salvation unfolds, God always grants us the capacity to respond and, if we choose to utilize it, moves us further along in the journey of faith. United Methodism is characterized by a theology of grace that emphasizes God's free gift of salvation to all who will accept it. Grace is manifested in our lives in several functions, according to our needs.

We believe that God channels divine grace to us through a variety of means or instruments that God has chosen. A metaphor that might be helpful is that of the wind, which blows anywhere and everywhere. There are, though, certain winds known to blow consistently—trade winds. In

areas where the trade winds blow, the wind is to be expected; it can be counted on. So can be the means of grace. The church itself is sacramental; it is the community designated and empowered by God to carry forward the divine work of redeeming the world. It is truly the body of Christ—continuing Christ's work of healing, reconciliation, and justice. Although God is supremely free and works beyond, and sometimes in spite of, the church, still the church is the community of grace. The sacraments are given to the church and can be understood as especially potent means of grace. God has chosen to use natural elements of water, bread, and wine as vehicles of grace when they are employed in the sacramental services of the church. When we participate in baptism and Holy Communion, we can be assured that grace is active and accessible.

While there is no fully developed theology of Holy Communion laid out in the New Testament, several major themes are present—Thanksgiving, fellowship, remembrance, sacrifice, action of the Holy Spirit, and eschatology.[1] All of these contribute to our understanding of the sacrament today. The theme of thanksgiving has become more prominent in recent decades, as evidenced by more frequent use of the name *Eucharist* for the sacrament. The Services of Word and Table in the 1989 *Hymnal* have a tone of celebratory gratitude much more than did those rituals used previously. The word *communion* means intimate fellowship and sharing. In Holy Communion we experience such fellowship with Christ, with the whole gathered congregation, with the body of Christ universal, and with those who have passed into the life beyond. In the sacrament, we rehearse the history of God's work for our salvation, culminating in the death and resurrection of Christ. These events become

expounded. The Supper of the Lord. Family and private prayer. Searching the Scriptures. Fasting or abstinence" (*BOD*; ¶ 103, page 74).

Elsewhere Wesley added Christian conferencing, by which he meant edifying conversation and meeting together in groups for nurture and accountability. These means are not to be understood as ways of earning salvation, for that is an unmerited gift. They are, rather, ways to receive, live in, and grow in divine grace. The Wesleyan tradition has continued to emphasize the practice of these means of grace throughout our salvation process.

## The Theology of Sacraments

The Greek word used in the early church for sacrament is *mysterion*, usually translated mystery. It indicates that through sacraments, God discloses things that are beyond human capacity to know through reason alone. In Latin the word used is *sacramentum*, which means a vow or promise. The sacraments were instituted by Christ and given to the church. Jesus Christ is himself the ultimate manifestation of a sacrament. In the coming of Jesus of Nazareth, God's nature and purpose were revealed and active through a human body. The Christian church is also sacramental. It was instituted to continue the work of Christ in redeeming the world. The church is Christ's body—the visible, material instrument through which Christ continues to be made known and the divine plan is fulfilled. Holy Baptism and Holy Communion have been chosen and designated by God as special means through which divine grace comes to us. Holy Baptism is the sacrament that initiates us into the body of Christ "through water and the Spirit"[2] (*UMH*; page 37). In baptism we receive our identity and mission as Christians. Holy Communion is the sacrament that sustains and nourishes us in our journey of salvation. In a sacrament, God uses tangible, material things as vehicles or instruments of grace. Wesley defines a sacrament, in accord with his Anglican tradition, as "an outward sign of inward grace, and a means whereby we receive the same."[3] Sacraments are sign-acts, which include words, actions, and physical elements. They both express and convey the gracious love of God. They make God's love both visible and effective. We might even say that sacraments are God's "show and tell," communicating with us in a way that we, in all our brokenness and limitations, can receive and experience God's grace.

## The Meaning of Holy Communion

In the New Testament, at least six major ideas about Holy Communion are present: thanksgiving, fellowship, remembrance, sacrifice, action of the Holy Spirit, and eschatology. A brief look at each of these will help us better comprehend the meaning of the sacrament.

Holy Communion is Eucharist, an act of thanksgiving. The early Christians "broke bread in their homes and ate together with glad and sincere hearts, praising God and enjoying the favor of all the people"[4] (Acts 2:46-47a, *NIV*). As we commune, we express joyful thanks for God's mighty acts throughout history—for creation, covenant, redemption, sanctification. The Great Thanksgiving ("A Service of Word and Table I," *UMH*; pages 9–10) is a recitation of this salvation history, culminating in the work of Jesus Christ and the ongoing work of the Holy Spirit. It conveys our gratitude for the goodness of God and God's unconditional love for us.

Holy Communion is the communion of the church—the gathered community of the faithful, both local and universal. While deeply meaningful to the individuals participating, the sacrament is much more than a personal event. The first-person pronouns throughout the ritual are consistently plural—*we, us, our*. First Corinthians 10:17 explains that "because there is one bread, we who are many are one body, for we all partake of the one bread." "A Service of Word and Table I" uses this text as an explicit statement of Christian unity in the body of Christ (*UMH*; page 11). The sharing and bonding experienced at the Table exemplify the nature of the church and model the world as God would have it be.

Holy Communion is remembrance, commemoration, and memorial, but this remembrance is much more than simply intellectual recalling. "Do this in remembrance of me" (Luke 22:19; 1 Corinthians 11:24-25) is *anamnesis* (the biblical Greek word). This dynamic action becomes re-presentation of past gracious acts of God in the present, so powerfully as to make them truly present now. Christ is risen and is alive here and now, not just remembered for what was done in the past.

Holy Communion is a type of sacrifice. It is a re-presentation, not a repetition, of the sacrifice of Christ. Hebrews 9:26 makes clear that "he has appeared once for all at the end of the age to remove sin by the sacrifice of himself." Christ's atoning life, death, and resurrection make divine grace available to us. We also present ourselves as sacrifice in union with Christ (Romans 12:1; 1 Peter 2:5) to be used by God

so powerfully real to us that it is as if we were actually experiencing them here and now. The theme of sacrifice reminds us that through the atoning death of Christ our salvation is made possible. In response we offer our own lives as a sacrifice in service to God. It is through the work of the Holy Spirit that these sacramental themes are made known to us, that we meet Christ at the table and receive the spiritual benefits made available there. Our church is regaining its sense of the sacrament as prolepsis or anticipation, offering such a vivid glimpse of life in the heavenly kingdom that we experience that life now, although fleetingly. This theme of future hope is important in a world of violence and alienation.

We come to the Table of the Lord seeking to have our spiritual needs met as we enjoy a richer sacramental life. These benefits include forgiveness, nourishment, healing, transformation, ministry and mission, and eternal life. To meditate on the significance of these spiritual benefits is to realize how superficial and narrow our expectations often are as we partake of Holy Communion.

## Teaching and Learning

### Resources and Materials

- Copies of *The United Methodist Hymnal*
- Copies of *The Book of Discipline—2004*
- Bibles
- *Quarterly Review*, Fall 2002
- *Sacraments as God's Self-Giving: Sacramental Practice and Faith*, by James F. White
- Markerboard or newsprint and markers
- *Eucharist and Eschatology*, by Geoffrey Wainwright

1. Identify and discuss the meanings of the various aspects of grace that are mentioned on pages 15–16. Choose familiar hymns from the "The Power of the Holy

Spirit" section of the *Hymnal* (pages 328–336) and look in them for references to how grace works in our lives.

2. Read John Wesley's General Rules in the *Discipline* (pages 72–74) to see how Wesley treats the importance of the means of grace. What experiences have you had in practicing these means?

3. Discuss: How should we understand the nature and function of the church? How does church as community that regularly gathers around the Table affect your thinking about church life, worship, and mission?

4. Discuss: What is meant by calling the sacraments a kind of divine "show and tell"?

5. Read aloud the biblical references cited for the New Testament meanings of Holy Communion (pages 17–18) and discuss their meaning. How does this material relate to our understandings of the sacrament today? Find places in "A Service of Word and Table I" (*The United Methodist Hymnal*, pages 6–11, and Appendix in this study guide) that express the various themes mentioned here and elsewhere.

6. Find places in "A Service of Word and Table I" that relate to the spiritual benefits to be gained by partaking of Holy Communion. Ask participants to tell about times when they have been aware of experiencing some or all of these benefits.

*7. Assign in advance sections of Karen B. Westerfield Tucker's "'Let Us Thy Mercy Prove': A United Methodist Understanding of the Eucharist" (*Quarterly Review*, Fall 2002, pages 234–247). Ask participants to present these sections and lead discussion on them in the session.

in the work of redemption, reconciliation, and justice. In the Great Thanksgiving, the church prays: "We offer ourselves in praise and thanksgiving as a holy and living sacrifice, in union with Christ's offering for us . . ."[5] (*UMH*; page 10).

Holy Communion is a vehicle of God's grace through the action of the Holy Spirit (Acts 1:8), whose work is described in John 14:26: "But the Advocate, the Holy Spirit, whom the Father will send in my name, will teach you everything, and remind you of all that I have said to you." The epiclesis (biblical Greek meaning "calling upon") is the part of the Great Thanksgiving that calls the Spirit: "Pour out your Holy Spirit on us gathered here, and on these gifts of bread and wine." The church asks God to make them be for us the body and blood of Christ, that we may be for the world the body of Christ, redeemed by his blood. By your Spirit make us one with Christ, one with each other, and one in ministry to all the world . . ."[6] (*UMH*; page 10).

Holy Communion is eschatological, meaning that it has to do with the end of history, the outcome of God's purpose for the world: "Christ has died; Christ is risen; Christ will come again"[7] (*UMH*; page 10). We commune not only with the faithful who are physically present but with the saints of the past who join us in the sacrament. To participate is to receive a foretaste of the future, a pledge of heaven "until Christ comes in final victory and we feast at his heavenly banquet"[8] (*UMH*; page 10). Christ himself looked forward to this occasion and promised the disciples, "I will never again drink of this fruit of the vine until that day when I drink it new with you in my Father's kingdom" (Matthew 26:29; Mark 14:25; Luke 22:18). When we eat and drink at the Table, we become partakers of the divine nature in this life and for life eternal (John 6:47-58; Revelation 3:20). We are anticipating the heavenly banquet celebrating God's victory over sin, evil, and death (Matthew 22:1-14; Revelation 19:9; 21:1-7). In the midst of the personal and systemic brokenness in which we live, we yearn for everlasting fellowship with Christ and ultimate fulfillment of the divine plan. Nourished by sacramental grace, we strive to be formed into the image of Christ and to be made instruments for transformation in the world.

## Toward a Richer Sacramental Life

Like the little girl who was disappointed with what she received, United Methodist people are looking and hoping for something more in their Eucharistic experience. As we move toward a richer sacramental life, including weekly celebration of Holy Communion, we ask what spiritual benefits we receive from it. What do divine love and power do in and for us through our participation in the sacrament? The answers to this question involve forgiveness, nourishment, healing, transformation, ministry and mission, and eternal life.

We respond to the invitation to the Table by immediately confessing our personal and corporate sin, trusting that, "If we confess our sins, he who is faithful and just will forgive us our sins and cleanse us from all unrighteousness" (1 John 1:9). Our expression of repentance is answered by the absolution in which forgiveness is proclaimed: "In the name of Jesus Christ, you are forgiven!"[9] (*UMH*; page 8). This assurance is God's gift to sinners, enabling us to continue striving to live faithfully. Wesley wrote, "The grace of God given herein confirms to us the pardon of our sins, and enables us to leave them."[10]

We receive spiritual nourishment through Holy Communion. The Christian life is a journey, one that is challenging and arduous. To continue living faithfully and growing in holiness requires constant sustenance. Wesley wrote, "This is the food of our souls: This gives strength to perform our duty, and leads us on to perfection."[11] God makes such sustenance available through the sacrament of Eucharist. In John 6:35, Jesus tells the crowd: "I am the bread of life. Whoever comes to me will never be hungry, and whoever believes in me will never be thirsty." As we return to the Table again and again, we are strengthened repeatedly. We go out empowered to live as disciples, reconcilers, and witnesses. In the words of the prayer after Communion, "Grant that we may go into the world in the strength of your Spirit, to give ourselves for others"[12] (*UMH*; page 11).

As we encounter Christ in Holy Communion and are repeatedly touched by divine grace, we are progressively shaped into Christ's image. All of this work is not done in a moment, no matter how dramatic an experience we may enjoy. It is, instead, a lifelong process through which God intends to shape us into people motivated by love, empowered and impassioned to do Christ's work in the world. The identity and ministry that God bestows on us in our baptism are fulfilled as we continue to be transformed into disciples who can respond to God's love by loving God and others (Romans 12:1-2).

Through Eucharist, we receive healing and are enabled to aid in the healing of others. *Sozo*, the root of the Greek word used in the New Testament for "healing," is also translated as "salvation" and

## To Expand the Study
### (for clergy and in academic settings)

1. Using the "Wesleyan Way or Order of Salvation," page 63 of this study guide, discuss Wesley's understanding of the salvation process. What aspects of grace are involved? What part do the sacraments of baptism and Holy Communion play throughout the journey of faith?

*2. Ask participants to read in advance chapters 1 and 3 of James F. White's *Sacraments as God's Self-Giving: Sacramental Practice and Faith* and discuss them together.

3. Compile a list of the hymns most frequently used in your congregations when the Lord's Supper is celebrated. Examine these hymns to find references to the New Testament themes and the spiritual benefits of the sacrament. Which themes and spiritual benefits are neglected?

*4. Ask participants to read in advance pages 25–42, 60–68, and 119–122 (at least) in Geoffrey Wainwright's *Eucharist and Eschatology*, and discuss them together in the session.

5. Outline a series of sermons that would convey to your congregations the material in this session. Develop these sermons as far as time allows and talk with one another about what approaches each sermon would take.

## Endnote

1 The ideas in this paragraph are drawn from the works of James F. White and Laurence Hull Stookey.

"wholeness." Much of this healing is spiritual, but it also includes the healing of our thoughts and emotions, of our minds and bodies, of our attitudes and relationships. The grace received at the Table of the Lord can make us whole. As those who are being saved, we seek to bring healing to a broken world. *The United Methodist Book of Worship* describes this well:

> Spiritual healing is God's work of offering persons balance, harmony, and wholeness of body, mind, spirit, and relationships through confession, forgiveness, and reconciliation. Through such healing, God works to bring about reconciliation between God and humanity, among individuals and communities, within each person, and between humanity and the rest of creation.[13] (Page 613)

Holy Communion can be a powerful aspect of the services of healing provided in the *Book of Worship* (pages 615–623).

The grace we receive at the Lord's Table enables us to perform our ministry and mission, to continue his work in the world—the work of redemption, reconciliation, peace, and justice (2 Corinthians 5:17-21). As we commune, we become aware of the worth and the needs of other people and are reminded of our responsibility. We express the compassion of Christ through acts of caring and kindness toward those we encounter in our daily lives. In our baptism, we have vowed to "accept the freedom and power God gives [us] to resist evil, injustice, and oppression in whatever forms they present themselves"[14] (*UMH*; page 34). But, in the words of the prayer of confession, we acknowledge our failures: "We have rebelled against your love, we have not loved our neighbors, and we have not heard the cry of the needy"[15] (*UMH*; page 8). Remembering the revolutionary Jesus, we are impelled to challenge unjust practices and systems that perpetuate political, economic, and social inequity and discrimination (Matthew 23; Luke 4:16-21; 14:7-11).

The loving God who meets us at the Table gives us the gift of eternal life. Jesus' presentation of himself as the spiritual bread of life in John's Eucharistic account (6:25-58) makes clear the connection: "Those who eat my flesh and drink my blood have eternal life, and I will raise them up on the last day" (6:54). This life in union with Christ is life eternal. It is not only the promise of our being with Christ after physical death. It is also our being in dynamic loving relationship with Christ here and now. It is life that never ends because it is grounded in the everlasting love of God who comes to us in the sacraments.

O Thou who this mysterious bread
didst in Emmaus break,
return, herewith our souls to feed,
and to thy followers speak.

Charles Wesley
*The United Methodist Hymnal,* 613

## Endnotes

1 From "The Means of Grace," II.1.

2 From "Baptismal Covenant I," © 1976, 1980, 1985, 1989 The United Methodist Publishing House.

3 From "The Means of Grace," II.1.

4 From the Holy Bible, NEW INTERNATIONAL VERSION®. Copyright © 1973, 1978, 1984 International Bible Society. All rights reserved throughout the world. Used by permission of International Bible Society.

5 From "A Service of Word and Table I," © 1972, 1980, 1985, 1989 The United Methodist Publishing House.

6 From "A Service of Word and Table I."

7 Text of "Christ has died..." from *The Roman Missal,* © 1973 International Committee on English in the Liturgy, Inc. All rights reserved.

8 From "A Service of Word and Table I."

9 From "A Service of Word and Table I."

10 From "The Duty of Constant Communion," I.3.

11 From "The Duty of Constant Communion," I.3.

12 From "A Service of Word and Table I."

13 From *The United Methodist Book of Worship,* © 1992 The United Methodist Publishing House.

14 From "Baptismal Covenant I."

15 From "A Service of Word and Table I."

## Part Two: Christ Is Here: Experiencing the Mystery

### The Presence of Christ

#### Principle:

Jesus Christ, who "is the reflection of God's glory and the exact imprint of God's very being" (Hebrews 1:3), is truly present in Holy Communion. Through Jesus Christ and in the power of the Holy Spirit, God meets us at the Table. God, who has given the sacraments to the church, acts in and through Holy Communion. Christ is present through the community gathered in Jesus' name (Matthew 18:20), through the Word proclaimed and enacted, and through the elements of bread and wine shared (1 Corinthians 11:23-26). The divine presence is a living reality and can be experienced by participants; it is not a remembrance of the Last Supper and the Crucifixion only.

#### Background:

Christ's presence in the sacrament is a promise to the church and is not dependent upon recognition of this presence by individual members of the congregation. Holy Communion always offers grace. We are reminded of what God has done for us in the past, experience what God is doing now as we partake, and anticipate what God will do in the future work of salvation. "We await the final moment of grace, when Christ comes in victory at the end of the age to bring all who are in Christ into the glory of that victory" ("By Water and the Spirit," *BOR*, page 857), and we join in feasting at the heavenly banquet table (Luke 22:14-18; Revelation 19:9).

For many United Methodists, the remembrance or memorial aspect of the Eucharist is the sole, or at least prime, meaning that they recognize. But Holy Communion involves much more. A sacrament is a sign-act in which God uses the tangible and material as vehicle for spiritual grace. In Holy Communion, Jesus Christ, through the power of the Holy Spirit, is truly present with and for the church. Christ's presence is not limited to particular words or actions or objects; it is in the totality of the experience. The presence is not physical; Christ cannot be seen or touched, but Christ can be perceived and experienced by those who come to the Table.

The divine presence is not in the elements of bread and wine (as we often understand Roman Catholicism to teach). Neither does the reality of the presence depend upon the faith of the worshipers, a view called receptionism. The presence is an act of God and is objective, existing independently of any human thought or act. This truth is a mystery; it is far beyond our human capacity to grasp or explain. Jewish and Christian practices, though, shape our ways of entering into the mystery of God's sacramental practice. Perhaps it will be helpful to us that in the post-modern world of the twenty-first century, our ways of perceiving reality are changing. The eighteenth-century Enlightenment determined western civilization's ways of knowing for centuries. In the

contemporary world, dependence upon reason is gradually being supplemented by a recognition, even in the scientific community, that much reality is indeterminate and inexplicable. It is not just in matters of faith that we must accept mysteriousness.

Christ is the host who invites us to the Table. Therefore, we need to be careful in imposing our own views as to who is eligible to come. Historically, baptized Christians have been considered members of the body of Christ and, therefore, qualified to eat the meal of the Christian community. Many branches of Christianity require baptism, and some insist upon the test of an acceptable moral life. John Wesley issued tickets or tokens that allowed some of the early Methodists to commune and, at least temporarily, barred others. Methodism in America exists in a different environment and has moved in another direction. During the nineteenth century, keen competition existed between Methodists and Baptists, especially on the ever-moving frontier. Most Baptist groups practiced what they called "close Communion," limiting access to the Table to those who had been immersed. Methodists reacted strongly against that position and through the years have come to value deeply "the open table." For many it became an identifying mark of Methodism, a hallmark of the denomination.

This does not mean that the Table is open to any who might choose to partake for whatever reason. Pastors need to be more specific than simply announcing that all are welcome. The Table is open to those who come to seek Christ's grace, who are moved by the Holy Spirit. The Table is open to any who honestly respond to the invitation as given in the ritual. For this reason, it is important that every Eucharistic service include that invitation, perhaps with addi-

The Christian church has struggled through the centuries to understand just how Christ is present in the Eucharist. Arguments and divisions have occurred over the matter. The Wesleyan tradition affirms the reality of Christ's presence, although it does not claim to be able to explain it fully. John and Charles Wesley's 166 *Hymns on the Lord's Supper* are our richest resource for study in order to appreciate the Wesleyan understanding of the presence of Christ in the Eucharist. One of these hymns expresses well both the reality and the mystery:

> O the depth of love divine,
> the unfathomable grace!
> Who shall say how bread and wine
> God into us conveys!
> How the bread his flesh imparts,
> how the wine transmits his blood,
> fills his faithful people's hearts
> with all the life of God!
>
> Sure and real is the grace,
> the manner be unknown;
> only meet us in thy ways
> and perfect us in one.
> Let us taste the heavenly powers,
> Lord, we ask for nothing more.
> Thine to bless, 'tis only ours
> to wonder and adore. (*UMH*, 627)

Article XVI of The Articles of Religion of The Methodist Church describes the sacraments as "certain signs of grace, and God's good will toward us, by which he doth work invisibly in us, and doth not only quicken, but also strengthen and confirm, our faith in him" (*BOD*; page 63).

Article XVIII describes the Lord's Supper as "a sacrament of our redemption by Christ's death; insomuch that, to such as rightly, worthily, and with faith receive the same, the bread which we break is a partaking of the body of Christ; and likewise the cup of blessing is a partaking of the blood of Christ" (*BOD*; page 64. See section "The Communion Elements" in this paper for related material.).

Article VI of The Confession of Faith of The Evangelical United Brethren Church speaks similarly of the sacraments: "They are means of grace by which God works invisibly in us, quickening, strengthening and confirming our faith in him. . . . Those who rightly, worthily and in faith eat the broken bread and drink the blessed cup partake of the body and blood of Christ in a spiritual manner until he comes" (*BOD*; page 68).

United Methodists, along with other Christian traditions, have tried to provide clear and faithful interpretations of Christ's presence in the Holy Meal. Our tradition asserts the real, personal, living presence of Jesus Christ. For United Methodists, the Lord's Supper is anchored in the life of the historical Jesus of Nazareth but is not primarily a remembrance or memorial. We do not embrace the medieval doctrine of transubstantiation, though we do believe that the elements are essential tangible means through which God works. We understand the divine presence in temporal and relational terms. In the Holy Meal of the church, the past, present, and future of the living Christ come together by the power of the Holy Spirit so that we may receive and embody Jesus Christ as God's saving gift for the whole world.

### Practice:

Because Jesus Christ has promised to meet us there (1 Corinthians 11:23-26), Christians approach the Communion Table with desire and expectation, with awe and humility, and with celebration and gratitude.

Pastors need to be trained and formed (in seminary, course of study, licensing school, and continuing education) in the theology, spirituality, history, and tradition of the sacraments and in how to most effectively utilize proclamation, ritual, gestures, postures, and material signs in order to convey their full meaning.

## Christ Is Calling You

### Invitation to the Lord's Table

### Principle:

The invitation to the Table comes from the risen and present Christ. Christ invites to his Table those who love him, repent of sin, and seek to live as Christian disciples. Holy Communion is a gift of God to the church and an act of the community of faith. By responding to this invitation we affirm and deepen our personal relationship with God through Jesus Christ and our commitment to membership and mission in the body of Christ.

### Background:

The Invitation to Holy Communion in "A Service of Word and Table I" and "A Service of Word and Table II" proclaims, "Christ our Lord invites to his table all who love him, who earnestly repent of their sin and seek to live in peace with one another"[1] (*UMH*; pages 7, 12). The more traditional wording in "A Service of Word and Table IV" invites, "Ye that do truly and earnestly repent of your sins, and are in love and

tional explanation. The purpose is not to clarify conditions that may cause a person to be barred from receiving; there may be no such conditions. The purpose is, instead, to communicate something of the significance and power of the sacrament. People should not be encouraged to participate casually or thoughtlessly. The invitation is not just to a meal; it is to a life. The invitation should be followed by confession of sin and receiving of pardon in preparation for partaking.

It is essential that we recognize and teach the intimate relationship between the two sacraments. Baptism signals the initiation of a person into the church and incorporates an individual into the body of Christ. In baptism, recognize that we are claimed by God and made a part of the community of faith. Holy Communion is the sacred meal of that community of faith, celebrated in eating and drinking with one another and with Christ. Eucharist nourishes and sustains Christians as we continue striving to live as the people that God told us in baptism we are. The two sacraments are closely linked. This relationship could be meaningfully communicated if we followed the rubric in our Services of the Baptismal Covenant and continued every service of baptism with celebration of Holy Communion. The membership in the church of baptized infants, children, youth, and adults should be ritualized by their reception of the Eucharist immediately after baptism and on subsequent occasions when the congregation celebrates the sacrament.

The open Table signals Methodism's unwillingness to judge who is qualified to commune with Christ. Qualifications or worthiness to partake are irrelevant because we all stand in need of the divine grace made available to us in the sacrament. There are some people who believe that they need to be especially "good"—to have achieved an

admirable degree of holiness—before they are worthy of participating in the Lord's Supper. This idea is false and damaging. Not only does it express misunderstanding of the sacrament, but it also implies that salvation is attained through our own efforts. People with this view often feel that they must "try harder" to be who God wants them to be. The beauty of Holy Communion is its availability to all who need its grace. Those who feel unworthy are likely to be those who are most conscientious and most humble. They need to be assured that Christ beckons them to the Table.

## Teaching and Learning

### Resources and Materials

- *Sunday Dinner: The Lord's Supper and the Christian Life*, by William H. Willimon
- Copies of *The United Methodist Hymnal*
- *Quarterly Review*, Fall 2002
- *Sacraments and Discipleship: Understanding Baptism and the Lord's Supper in a United Methodist Context*, by Mark W. Stamm
- *Worship Matters: A United Methodist Guide to Ways to Worship, Volume 1*, E. Byron Anderson, editor

1. Notice that the remainder of the document is organized into principles, backgrounds, and practices as explained on page 9.

*2. Read in advance "The Real Presence," pages 28–33 in William H. Willimon's *Sunday Dinner: The Lord's Supper and the Christian Life*.

3. Discuss: How does the realization that Christ is truly present affect your view and practice of the Lord's Supper? Tell one another your experiences of Christ's sacramental presence.

charity with your neighbors, and intend to lead a new life, following the commandments of God, and walking from henceforth in his holy ways: Draw near with faith . . ."[2] (*UMH*; page 26). "A Service of Word and Table V," for use with people who are sick or homebound, says that Christ invites "all who love him and seek to grow into his likeness"[3] (*BOW*; page 51).

### Practice:

When Holy Communion is celebrated, it is important to always begin with the words of Invitation, including Confession and Pardon. If these are omitted, all those present may not understand either the openness of the Table of the Lord or the expectation of repentance, forgiveness, healing, and entrance into new life in Christ.

The church community has a responsibility to provide ongoing age-appropriate nurture and education about the sacrament of Holy Communion to all its people. Those who are baptized as infants need continual teaching as they mature in faith. Those who come into membership later in life also need ongoing instruction about the significance of the sacrament in their personal faith journey and in the life of the congregation and larger Christian community. All who seek to live as Christian disciples need formation in sacramental spirituality.

Bishops, elders, deacons, pastors, Sunday school teachers, parents and guardians, seminary professors, and others have responsibility for faithfully teaching understandings and practices of Holy Communion. Teaching about the sacraments should emphasize United Methodist positions and practices but should also encourage knowledge of and respect for those of other Christian traditions.

### Principle:

All who respond in faith to the invitation are to be welcomed. Holy Baptism normally precedes partaking of Holy Communion. Holy Communion is a meal of the community who are in covenant relationship with God through Jesus Christ. As circumcision was the sign of the covenant between God and the Hebrew people, baptism is the sign of the new covenant (Genesis 17:9-14; Exodus 24:1-12; Jeremiah 31:31; Romans 6:1-11; Hebrews 9:15).

### Background:

Baptism is the non-repeatable rite of initiation into the body of Christ, while the Lord's Supper is the regularly-repeated celebration of communion of the body of Christ.

Beginning early in its history, the Christian church divided its worship services into the Liturgy of the Word, in which all participated, and the Liturgy of the Faithful, which was the celebration of Holy Communion. Those who were not yet baptized were dismissed before the celebration of the sacrament (*Didache*, 9; Justin Martyr, *First Apology*, 66; *The Apostolic Constitutions*, Book VIII.VI; *The Liturgy of St. Basil*).

John Wesley stressed that baptism is only a step in the salvation process and must be followed by justifying faith and personal commitment to Christ when one reaches an age of accountability. He referred to Holy Communion as "a converting ordinance."[4] In eighteenth-century England, Wesley was addressing people who, for the most part, although baptized as infants and possessing some degree of faith, had not yet experienced spiritual rebirth. Therefore, the conversion Wesley spoke of was transformation of lives and assurance of salvation.

Soon after the merger of The Evangelical Church and the United Brethren in Christ, the Evangelical United Brethren *Discipline* of 1947, read, "We invite to [the Lord's Supper] all disciples of the Lord Jesus Christ who have confessed him before men and desire to serve him with sincere hearts."[5]

*The United Methodist Book of Worship* (page 29) says, "All who intend to lead a Christian life, together with their children, are invited to receive the bread and cup. We have no tradition of refusing any who present themselves desiring to receive"[6] (page 29). This statement means that in practice there are few, if any, circumstances in which a United Methodist pastor would refuse to serve the elements of Holy Communion to a person who comes forward to receive.

"By Water and the Spirit" affirms: "Because the table at which we gather belongs to the Lord, it should be open to all who respond to Christ's love, regardless of age or church membership. The Wesleyan tradition has always recognized that Holy Communion may be an occasion for the reception of converting, justifying, and sanctifying grace" (*BOR*; pages 873–874).

### Practice:

Invitation to partake of Holy Communion offers an evangelical opportunity to bring people into a fuller living relationship with the body of Christ. As means of God's unmerited grace, Holy Baptism and Holy Communion are to be seen not as barriers but as pathways. Pastors and congregations must strive for a balance of welcome that is open and gracious, and teaching that is clear and faithful to the fullness of discipleship.

4. Read all stanzas of Hymn No. 627, "O the Depth of Love Divine," and paraphrase them into more understandable language. Discuss Wesley's insistence on both the real presence of Christ and the utter mystery of it.

5. Discuss: What are some nonverbal ways that the presiding pastor can express the real presence? What might the congregation do? the altar guild?

6. Discuss the meaning of the sentence, "Holy Communion always offers grace" ("Background," page 23).

7. Examine and compare the three invitations from our ritual that are quoted in the Background section on pages 25–26. What do these invitations ask of every person who comes to the table?

*8. Assign in advance sections of Mark W. Stamm's "Open Communion as a United Methodist Exception" (*Quarterly Review*, Fall 2002, pages 261–272). Ask participants to present and lead discussion.

9. Consider this comment by William H. Willimon in *Sunday Dinner: The Lord's Supper and the Christian Life*, page 79: "I'm glad Judas was at the table with him that dark Thursday night, and Peter and all the rest. For if they had not been there then, I don't know how I could dare, my unfaithfulness being what it is, to come to the Lord's table on Sunday morning."[1] How would you answer a person who says: "I'm not worthy yet to take Communion"?

10. Discuss: *By Water and the Spirit, The Book of Discipline—2004* (¶ 215), and the services of Baptismal Covenant in the *Hymnal* make it clear that all those who are baptized, regardless of age, are members of the church. How might this understanding affect our practices

regarding children and the Lord's Supper?

11. Discuss: What education in the meaning of Eucharist needs to be given to children? to youth? to adults? Describe the kinds of experiences that enable people to appreciate the sacrament.

## To Expand the Study

### *(for clergy and in academic settings)*

1. Discuss what you were taught in your theological training about the presence of Christ in the Eucharist.

2. Discuss what words, actions, and attitudes would enable you as the presiding minister to help your congregation experience Christ's presence in the Lord's Supper.

3. Discuss how you as pastor can communicate clearly what the invitation to the Table is and is not.

4. Discuss: What do you see as your responsibilities in the sacramental education of your congregations? How are you fulfilling those responsibilities?

*5. Have participants read in advance pages 89–104 in Mark W. Stamm's *Sacraments and Discipleship: Understanding Baptism and the Lord's Supper in a United Methodist Context*, and pages 137–146 in Susan J. White's "Who Gets Communion?" in *Worship Matters: A United Methodist Guide to Ways to Worship, Volume 1.* Have them discuss their ideas in the session.

## Endnote

1 *Sunday Dinner: The Lord's Supper and the Christian Life,* by William H. Willimon, © 1981 The Upper Room.

Nonbaptized people who respond in faith to the invitation in our liturgy will be welcomed to the Table. They should receive teaching about Holy Baptism as the sacrament of entrance into the community of faith—needed only once by each individual—and Holy Communion as the sacrament of sustenance for the journey of faith and growth in holiness—needed and received frequently. "Unbaptized persons who receive communion should be counseled and nurtured toward baptism as soon as possible" ("By Water and the Spirit," in *BOR*; page 874).

### Principle:

No one will be turned away from the Table because of age or "mental, physical, developmental, and/or psychological and neurological" capacity (*BOD*; ¶ 162.G) or because of any other condition that might limit his or her understanding or hinder his or her reception of the sacrament.

### Background:

According to "By Water and the Spirit,"

The services of the baptismal covenant appropriately conclude with Holy Communion, through which the union of the new member with the body of Christ is most fully expressed. Holy Communion is a sacred meal in which the community of faith, in the simple act of eating bread and drinking wine, proclaims and participates in all that God has done, is doing, and will continue to do for us in Christ. In celebrating the Eucharist, we remember the grace given to us in our baptism and partake of the spiritual food necessary for sustaining and fulfilling the promises of salvation. (*BOR*; page 873)

The concluding rubrics of the services make clear that this applies to people of all ages.

The theological basis for baptism of infants and people of varying abilities applies as well to their participation in Holy Communion:

Through the church, God claims infants as well as adults to be participants in the gracious covenant of which baptism is the sign. This understanding of the workings of divine grace also applies to persons who for reasons of disabilities or other limitations are unable to answer for themselves the questions of the baptismal ritual. While we may not be able to comprehend how God works in their lives, our faith teaches us that God's grace is sufficient for their needs and, thus, they are appropriate recipients of baptism.

("By Water and the Spirit," *BOR*; page 868)

Likewise, the grace given through Holy Communion is offered to the entire church, including those who are unable to respond for themselves. Children are members of the covenant community and partici-pants in the Lord's Supper.

### Practice:

Young children and people with handicapping or incapacitating con-ditions may need special consideration as the elements are served. Pastors and congregations should develop plans for providing assistance that maintains the dignity and affirms the worth of those receiving.

Children of all ages are welcome to the Table and are to be taught and led to interpret, appreciate, and participate in Holy Communion. Adults need training to help them explain the sacrament to children.

When worship spaces are constructed or renovated, attention needs to be given to providing physical access to the Communion Table for all.

### Principle:

The Lord's Supper in a United Methodist congregation is open to members of other United Methodist congregations and to Christians from other traditions.

### Background:

"A baptized or professing member of any local United Methodist church is a member of the global United Methodist connection and a member of the church universal" (BOD; ¶ 215.4).

The United Methodist Church recognizes that it is only one of the bodies that constitute the community of Christians. Despite our differ-ences, all Christians are welcome at the Table of the Lord.

### Practice:

As a part of the directions before the invitation, it is customary to announce that all Christians are welcome to participate in the sacra-ment in United Methodist congregations.

Response to the invitation is always voluntary, and care needs to be taken to ensure that no one feels pressured to participate or con-spicuous for not doing so.

When Holy Communion is served as part of a service of Christian marriage or a service of death and resurrection, "It is our tradition to invite all Christians to the Lord's table, and the invitation should be extended to everyone present; but there should be no pressure that would embarrass those who for whatever reason do not choose to receive Holy Communion"[7] (BOW; page 152). It is not appropriate for only the couple or family to commune.

## The Issue of "Unworthiness"

### *Principle:*

Any person who answers in faith the invitation "Christ our Lord invites to his table all who love him, who earnestly repent of their sin and seek to live in peace with one another"[8] (*UMH*; page 7) is worthy through Christ to partake of Holy Communion. Christians come to the Lord's Table in gratitude for Christ's mercy toward sinners. We do not share in Communion because of our worthiness; no one is truly worthy. We come to the Eucharist out of our hunger to receive God's gracious love, to receive forgiveness and healing.

### *Background:*

Some deeply committed United Methodist people who hesitate or even refuse to partake of Holy Communion do so because of their sense that they are unworthy. This problem is largely based upon misinterpretation and false fears. Within the United Methodist tradition, people who participate in the sacrament are assured of the forgiveness of their sins and of pardon through their participation in the Invitation and the Confession and Pardon.

Paul's words of warning in 1 Corinthians 11:27-32 have long been a source of confusion and concern. Some people are fearful of communing "in an unworthy manner" and, sometimes out of genuine Christian humility, believe that their participation would be improper. John Wesley addressed this problem: "God offers you one of the greatest mercies on this side of heaven, and commands you to accept it. . . . You are unworthy to receive any mercy from God. But is that a reason for refusing all mercy? . . . Why do you not obey God's command? . . . What! unworthy to obey God?"[9]

Wesley went on to explain that unworthiness applies not to the people who are to commune but to the manner in which the consecrated elements are consumed: "Here is not a word said of being unworthy to eat and drink. Indeed he [Paul] does speak of eating and drinking unworthily; but that is quite a different thing. . . . In this very chapter we are told that by eating and drinking unworthily is meant, taking the holy Sacrament in such a rude and disorderly way, that one was "hungry, and another drunken"[10] [1 Cor. 11:21].

First Corinthians 11:29 is a word of judgment against "all who eat and drink without discerning the body." A footnote to this passage in *The New Oxford Annotated Bible* (NRSV) explains that this is a reference to "the community, one's relation to other Christians."[11] Paul is

This Holy Mystery

speaking against those who fail to recognize the church—the body of Christ—as a community of faith within which Christians relate to one another in love.

### Practice:

Pastors and other leaders can alleviate most of these concerns about worthiness through patient counseling, faithful teaching, and prayers for healing. These efforts can be focused on study of the cited passage in First Corinthians, with clear explanation of what it meant in its first-century context and what it means today.

## Endnotes

1 From "A Service of Word and Table I and II," © 1972, 1980, 1985, 1989 The United Methodist Publishing House.

2 From "A Service of Word and Table IV," © 1957 Board of Publication, Evangelical United Brethren Church; © 1964, 1965, 1989 The United Methodist Publishing House.

3 From "A Service of Word and Table V," © 1976, 1980 by Abingdon; © 1985, 1987, 1992 UMPH.

4 From "Journal from November 1, 1739, to September 3, 1741," Friday, June 27, 1740.

5 From *The Discipline of The Evangelical United Brethren Church*, 1947, © UMPH; page 447.

6 From "An Order of Sunday Worship Using the Basic Pattern," © 1985, 1989, 1992 UMPH.

7 From "An Order for Holy Communion," © 1972 The Methodist Publishing House; © 1979, 1980, 1981, 1985, 1987, 1989, 1992 UMPH.

8 From "A Service of Word and Table I."

9 From "The Duty of Constant Communion," II.7–8.

10 From "The Duty of Constant Communion," II.8.

11 From *The New Oxford Annotated Bible*, © Oxford University Press; page 242.

## The Basic Pattern of Worship: A Service of Word and Table

### Principle:

The complete pattern of Christian worship for the Lord's Day is Word and Table—the gospel is proclaimed in both Word and sacrament. Word and Table are not in competition; rather they complement each other so as to constitute a whole service of worship. Their separation diminishes the fullness of life in the Spirit offered to us through faith in Jesus Christ.

### Background:

In *The United Methodist Book of Worship* (pages 13–14), the Basic Pattern of Worship is traced to its Jewish roots:

> The Entrance and the Proclamation and Response—often called the Service of the Word or the Preaching Service—are a Christian adaptation of the ancient synagogue service.
> The Thanksgiving and Communion, commonly called the Lord's Supper or Holy Communion, is a Christian adaptation of Jewish worship at family meal tables. . . .
> Christians held an adapted synagogue service and broke bread when they gathered on the first day of the week. (Acts 20:7)[1]

The practice of the Christian church from its earliest years was weekly celebration of the Lord's Supper on the Lord's Day. The *Didache*, a source from the late first century or early second century, says, "On every Lord's Day—his special day—come together and break bread and give thanks . . ."[2] Justin Martyr, writing around A.D. 150, relates, "And on the day called Sunday there is a meeting . . . bread is brought, and wine and water, and the president similarly sends up prayers and thanksgivings . . ."[3] Most Christian traditions have continued this pattern.

John Wesley was highly critical of the infrequency of Holy Communion in the Church of England of his day. He exhorted his followers to

Perhaps the most enthusiastic recommendation made by the committee that created "This Holy Mystery" is that congregations increase the frequency of their celebration of Holy Communion. Many congregations have already moved away from the old practice of quarterly Communion to a bimonthly or monthly pattern. Some are adding sacramental celebrations on special days in the Christian year such as Christmas (or Christmas Eve), Epiphany, Ash Wednesday, Holy Thursday, Easter, and Pentecost. Others are observing the Lord's Supper on the Sundays during special seasons such as Advent, Lent, or Eastertide. The goal is ultimately to offer the Eucharist weekly at Sunday services. This would be a reclamation of the fullness of Christian worship that includes both Word and Table.

Some people in our congregations—and some pastors—object to this increasing frequency. Perhaps the most common argument is that such repetition decreases appreciation of the sacrament or makes it have less special significance. These objections point to the need to enable people to experience the Eucharist as a life-sustaining occurrence, providing the strength and sustenance that allow us to continue our spiritual journeys. This is a challenge to those who plan and lead worship: to offer the sacrament in ways that make it deeply meaningful and therefore special every time it is administered, no matter how often.

Issues relating to the length of worship

services cannot be avoided. While it is easy to claim piously that worshipers should be willing to stay as long as necessary, it is not a realistic expectation. Clergy in multichurch appointments have to leave one worship service to go immediately to another. Services in many churches are broadcast or telecast and are abruptly truncated if they exceed the scheduled time. Serious attention must be given to use of time, including assessment of the various components of the service and ascertaining priorities. Every effort has to be made to present the service as an integration of Word and Table. The service of Table must not be treated or experienced as an addendum or appendix. Simple approaches can help, such as constructing the worship bulletin so that Word and Table have equal weight visually as well as theologically.

It needs to be apparent to congregations that Holy Communion is a celebration that includes all of the worshiping community. In the Anglican Church of Wesley's time, and in many other settings, priests were not to observe the sacrament by themselves. Pastors do not celebrate in the absence of a congregation. Neither are they, in corporate worship, the sole actors while the people watch passively. Pastors lead; congregations respond; both are essential. The Great Thanksgiving is a responsive prayer in which both pastor and people have their parts. Baptized Christians share in the ministry of the church, including that of sacrament. Almost surely, the enthusiasm of our people for regular, frequent services of Word and Table would be enhanced if they experienced themselves as active participants. Congregational singing has always been an important part of Wesleyan worship. One of the best ways to enhance the participation of the whole assembly in sacra-

practice "constant communion" because Christ had so commanded and because the spiritual benefits are so great.[4] In his 1784 letter to American Methodists, Wesley counseled, "I also advise the elders to administer the supper of the Lord on every Lord's day."[5]

For decades the scarcity of ordained pastors made it difficult if not impossible for churches in the Wesleyan tradition to observe the Lord's Supper as a part of regular Sunday worship. The custom of celebrating the sacrament at least quarterly, when an ordained elder was present, ensured the opportunity for regular if infrequent participation. With the introduction of new liturgical texts for the Lord's Supper in 1972, United Methodism has been recovering the fullness of Word and Table as the pattern for weekly worship on the Lord's Day.

The Journal of Christian Newcomer, third bishop of the United Brethren in Christ, is filled with references to frequent celebrations of Holy Communion. He rejoiced in the "sacramental festivals" that he led and in which he participated.

Recent theology and practice of worship stress both the proclamation of the gospel enacted through Holy Communion and the sacramental power of Christ's presence through preaching. Partaking of Holy Communion is a response to and continued participation in the Word that has been proclaimed. Those seeking to live as Christian disciples have constant need of the nourishment and sustenance made available through both the Word and the sacrament of Holy Communion.

### Practice:

Congregations of The United Methodist Church are encouraged to move toward a richer sacramental life, including weekly celebration of the Lord's Supper at the services on the Lord's Day, as advocated by the general orders of Sunday worship in *The United Methodist Hymnal* and *The United Methodist Book of Worship*. The sacrament can also be celebrated appropriately on other occasions in the life of the church from the congregational to the denominational level. However, occasions of worship that might not always include Communion are revivals, services of daily praise and prayer, love feasts, and services on days other than Sunday.

Attention should be given to the special needs of churches whose pastoral leadership is neither ordained nor licensed. Cooperative parishes and ecumenical shared ministries (*BOD*; ¶¶ 206.2 and 207) may offer patterns through which such congregations could receive regular sacramental ministry.

# The Gathered Community

## The Whole Assembly

### Principle:

The whole assembly actively celebrates Holy Communion. All who are baptized into the body of Christ Jesus become servants and ministers within that body, which is the church. The members are claimed by God as a royal priesthood, God's own people (1 Peter 2:9). The one body, drawn together by the one Spirit, is fully realized when all its many parts eat together in love and offer their lives in service at the Table of the Lord.

### Background:

Those baptized are called "Christ's royal priesthood"[6] in the United Methodist services of the Baptismal Covenant (*BOW*; page 92). We are "royal" because we belong to Christ, the sovereign. As priests, each of us can have access to God without any human intermediary. This priesthood means, especially, that we are to be priests to each other as together we seek to live as Christians. The exchange of words of forgiveness between pastor and congregation is an example in the ritual of this role (*UMH*; page 8).

All Christians share in the ministry of the church. Our diverse abilities and callings are gifts from God that together form the unity of the body of Christ and carry out its mission (Romans 12:3-8; 1 Corinthians 12:4-30; Ephesians 4:1-16). There is no more powerful expression of this reality than the participation of the whole gathered community in the celebration of Eucharist.

### Practice:

All in the congregation are participants in the ministry of offering praise and worship to God and in the servant work of mutual ministry. The terms *presiding minister* and *assisting minister* describe the work of those who lead and assist the congregation.

## The Prayer of Great Thanksgiving

### Principle:

The prayer of Great Thanksgiving is addressed to God, is prayed by the whole people, and is led by the presiding minister. The prayer is shaped by our Trinitarian understanding of the nature of God. It includes an introductory dialogue, thankful remembrance of God's mighty acts of creation and the salvation made possible through Jesus Christ, the institution of the Lord's Supper, invoking of the present work of the Holy Spirit, and concluding praise to the Trinity. The prayer

mental celebration is to use the Eucharistic hymns in *The United Methodist Hymnal* (Nos. 612–641) and *The Faith We Sing* (Nos. 2254–2269). Another factor in heightening the sense of participation is the sense of accessibility and relationship to the action. Any way of arranging space to give a sense of being *around* the table improves the experience of participation.

The Great Thanksgiving prayer is at the heart of the Eucharist. In the opening dialogue the presiding minister invokes God's grace for the people ("The Lord be with you") and the people invoke God's grace upon the presider to lead the people in the Eucharistic prayer ("And also with you").[1] The Great Thanksgiving is then a comprehensive narrative of the Christian understanding of God's work for salvation. The entire prayer is addressed to the first person of the Trinity, and the three main sections describe the saving work of Father, Son, and Holy Spirit. The first section praises God as creator and for the covenant relationship with Israel. The second focuses on the redeeming work of Christ. The third main section invokes the presence and work of the Holy Spirit. The prayer includes thanksgiving for the divine work of creation, summary of God's action in salvation history, Christ's institution of the Lord's Supper, invocation of the Holy Spirit, and praise of the triune God. When the church prays this prayer, it expresses, perhaps more profoundly than anywhere else, what it believes about Holy Communion. The Great Thanksgiving is a prayer of the entire gathered community, led by the presiding pastor with responses by the congregation, spoken or sung. The single word "Amen" is an important response because with it the congregation claims and affirms that the prayer is theirs.

Appropriate use of the creative arts enhances Eucharistic celebrations. Artistic presentations are to enrich the sacramental experience, not to be performances or ends unto themselves. Music may be used in several parts of the liturgy. There are several musical settings for The Great Thanksgiving, as well as for the "Kyrie Eleison" and the Lord's Prayer, in both *The United Methodist Hymnal* and *The Faith We Sing*. These may be in the form of call and response or in unison form with the leader and people together. Because the whole assembly should give voice to these responses, solo or ensemble singing should not be used. Another use of music might be to provide a soft continuous musical accompaniment over which the prayers and responses may be spoken. Such music may correspond to the liturgical season and the cultural setting. Music should not be used if it becomes a distraction. As the assembly is receiving the sacrament, congregational singing is desirable.

Visual art may be used to enhance the liturgical setting. Religious art such as paintings, sculpture, carvings, textiles, and so forth can be placed at or near the table. In churches equipped with video projection systems, traditional or abstract art, photography, and filmed segments can be projected and sequenced as appropriate. Organic materials are another way of enhancing the setting.

The church from its earliest days has mediated the gospel of Jesus Christ using the communications systems of the secular culture. The global culture of the twenty-first century is shifting from a print base to a digital media base. People are increasingly oriented to and hungry for story, experience, and divine beauty. In this emerging digital context, more and more churches are seeking to use digital technology in worship and out-

recognizes the fullness of God's triune nature, expresses the offering of ourselves in response, and looks toward the joy of sharing in God's eventual victory over sin and death.

### Background:

The Trinitarian structure is evident in the Great Thanksgiving in the Word and Table services of *The United Methodist Hymnal* (pages 6–16). Following the introductory exchange between presiding minister and people in the Great Thanksgiving, prayer is addressed to "Father [God] Almighty, creator of heaven and earth." Following the Sanctus ("Holy, holy, holy . . . " ), the work of the second person of the Trinity is proclaimed: ". . . and blessed is your Son [Child] Jesus Christ." The presence and work of the Holy Spirit are invoked in the portion beginning "Pour out your Holy Spirit on us gathered here and on these gifts . . . ,"[7] words historically known as the *epiclesis*. Throughout the Great Thanksgiving the congregation prays actively but silently and speaks its responses aloud at designated points in the service.

In their *Hymns on the Lord's Supper*, John and Charles Wesley make clear that divine presence and power come into the Eucharistic experience through the action of the Holy Spirit. Hymn 72 in that collection is a good example:

> Come, Holy Ghost, Thine influence shed,
> And realize [make real] the sign;
> Thy life infuse into the bread,
> Thy power into the wine.
> Effectual let the tokens prove,
> And made, by heavenly art,
> Fit channels to convey Thy love
> To every faithful heart.

Biblical worship was expressed in gestures and bodily movements, including bowing (Micah 6:6), lifting the cup of salvation (Psalm 116:13), lifting hands (Psalm 141:2), clapping (Psalm 47:1), and dancing (Psalm 149:3). The Gospels tell of Jesus' characteristic actions at meals that include taking bread, blessing or giving thanks, breaking the bread, and giving the bread. In Luke, the disciples who walked with Jesus on the way to Emmaus without recognizing him had their eyes opened "when he was at the table with them" and "he took bread, blessed and broke it, and gave it to them" (Luke 24:30).

### Practice:

The prayer of Great Thanksgiving includes the voices of both the presiding minister and the people. The congregation's responses, which may

This Holy Mystery

be spoken or sung, include adoration, acclamation, and affirmation.

The whole assembly might join in parts of the Great Thanksgiving that speak for them: (a) the memorial acclamation, beginning, "And so, in remembrance …"; (b) an expression of intention to serve the world, beginning, "Make them be for us …"; (c) the concluding doxology, beginning, "Through your Son Jesus Christ …"[8] (*UMH*; page 10). Congregational responses of "Amen" are the affirmation by the people of what has been prayed.

Presiding at Holy Communion involves bodily action as well as verbal communication. Gestures evoke and lead physical and visual participation by the congregation and aid worshipers in recognizing that the action at the Lord's Table is more than reading a script. For the presiding ministers, such gestures may include making welcoming gestures with arms or hands during the Invitation, raising arms or hands to God in praise or supplication, opening arms and hands to indicate including the entire body of Christ, and holding arms and hands over the elements as blessing.

Different postures are appropriate at different points in the ritual. The presiding minister and those in the whole assembly who are physically able appropriately stand throughout the Great Thanksgiving (*BOW*; page 28). Those unable to stand might participate with other gestures of praise as they desire. Standing communicates an attitude of respect and reverence; kneeling and bowing signify humility and confession; hands raised and open express praise and receptivity. The sign of the cross affirms our baptismal identity and the centrality of the cross to our faith. The ancient biblical use of hands and arms in expressing prayer and thanksgiving to God (arms uplifted, called *orans*; see 1 Timothy 2:8) and other gestures are recommended in *The United Methodist Book of Worship*, pages 36–39 and 46–79.

## The Community Extends Itself

### *Principle:*

The Communion elements are consecrated and consumed in the context of the gathered congregation. The Table may be extended, in a timely manner, to include those unable to attend because of age, illness, or similar conditions. Laypeople may distribute the consecrated elements in the congregation and extend them to members who are unavoidably absent (*BOD*; ¶¶ 340.2.*a*.5 and 1117.9). An elder or deacon should offer appropriate training, preparation, and supervision for this important task (¶¶ 340.2.*a*.5 and 1117.9).

reach. The incorporation of such technology is new for many and arouses concerns about cherished, familiar understandings and practices. Worship and communication media are inevitably changing, however, and churches are encouraged to engage congregations in sacramental worship using a faithful synthesis of oral, print, and digital/electronic cultures.

Probably in every congregation there are people who are unavoidably absent from services of worship and thus unable to receive Holy Communion with the gathered community. These people are not just those who are unable to leave their homes and attend public worship. They include the sick and injured, in hospital or home. They include those who are institutionalized in nursing homes, mental institutions, prisons and jails, and other settings. As the work schedules of many people are increasingly intruding into worship times, workers may be unable to join the gathered community. All these persons are members of the community of faith and could be offered the sacrament at another time and place. To fail to provide Communion is to deny our teaching about the significance of the Lord's Supper.

To provide such a broad Eucharistic ministry, both clergy and laypeople need to be involved as ministers. *The Book of Worship* provides "A Service of Word and Table IV" and "A Service of Word and Table V," both of which can be adapted for use on a variety of occasions. Clergy can use this shortened form when it is more appropriate than the whole service. If consecrated elements from the congregational celebration are used, the Great Thanksgiving is omitted. Laypeople can lead this shortened form of the service and serve consecrated elements without repeating the Great Thanksgiving. There is a distinction between reservation of the

consecrated elements, which United Methodists do not practice, and extension of the Table by serving consecrated elements in other settings. Such extension might be thought of as "the open table turned outward in pastoral care and mission."[2]

The ritual texts in *The United Methodist Hymnal* and *The United Methodist Book of Worship* are the culmination of a long process of development by the church. They draw upon the best of Christian tradition and authentically express the sacramental understandings of the church. These rituals are designed for rich and meaningful celebrations. Pastors are to utilize these rituals in their leadership of the Eucharist. This does not mean that there are no circumstances in which other rituals might be used or in which the creativity of leaders can be expressed. It does mean that pastors are not free to substitute their individual preferences and practices in the place of those instituted by the church.

## Teaching and Learning

### *Resources and Materials*

- Copies of *The United Methodist Book of Worship*
- Markerboard or newsprint and markers
- Copies of *The United Methodist Hymnal*
- *Worship Matters: A United Methodist Guide to Ways to Worship, Volume 1,* E. Byron Anderson, editor
- *Eucharist: Christ's Feast With the Church,* by Laurence Hull Stookey, including copies of pages 155–159
- *Creative Preaching on the Sacraments,* by Craig A. Satterlee and Lester Ruth
- "The Duty of Constant Communion," by John Wesley (in the Appendix of this study guide)

### *Background:*

In his description of worship practices of the early church, second-century writer Justin Martyr noted in his *First Apology* that consecrated bread and wine were carried to Christians who were unable to attend the service.

"Since the earliest Christian times, communion has been brought as an extension of the congregation's worship to sick or homebound persons unable to attend congregational worship"[9] (*BOW*; page 51).

### *Practice:*

When Holy Communion is extended to those unable to attend, the liturgy should include the reading of the Scripture Lesson(s), the Invitation, Confession and Pardon, the Peace, the Lord's Prayer, distribution, and post-Communion prayer. Elders, deacons, and laity may use this liturgy. A prayer of Great Thanksgiving should not be repeated, since this service is an extension of the Communion service held earlier (*BOW*; page 51).

If Holy Communion is to be celebrated with people who are homebound on a day when the congregation has not gathered at Table, "A Service of Word and Table V" (*BOW*; pages 51–53), which includes the Great Thanksgiving, should be used by an elder or another who is authorized to preside.

The Lord's Supper is to be made available to people who are in hospitals and hospices; nursing, convalescent, and rehabilitation facilities; correctional and custodial institutions; or other situations that make it impossible for them to gather with the community of faith. If a person is unable to eat or drink, one or both of the elements may be touched to his or her lips.

Both "self-service" Communion, where people help themselves, and "drop-in" Communion, where the elements are available over a period of time, are contrary to the communal nature of the sacrament, which is the celebration of the gathered community of faith.

## The Ritual of the Church

### *Principle:*

As stewards of the gifts given by God to the church, pastors have a responsibility to uphold and use the texts for Word and Table of The United Methodist Church found in *The United Methodist Hymnal; Mil Voces Para Celebrar: Himnario Metodista; Come, Let Us Worship: The Korean-English United Methodist Hymnal; The United Methodist Book of Worship;* and other liturgical material approved by central conferences in accordance with the *Book of Discipline,* ¶ 543.13. These liturgies, arising from biblical, historical, and ecumenical sources, are expressions of the Christian faith and the worship of God.

## Background:

Article XXII of The Articles of Religion of The Methodist Church affirms some diversity of "rites and ceremonies" but rebukes "whosoever, through his private judgment, willingly and purposely doth openly break the rites and ceremonies of the church" (BOD; page 65).

The Book of Discipline specifies in ¶ 1114.3 that

> the ritual of the Church is that contained in The United Methodist Hymnal (1989), The United Methodist Book of Worship (1992), Mil Voces Para Celebrar: Himnario Metodista (1996), and Come, Let Us Worship: The Korean-English United Methodist Hymnal (2000).

In the Order for the Ordination of Elders, candidates promise to "be loyal to The United Methodist Church, accepting its order, liturgy, doctrine, and discipline"[10] (BOW; page 676).

The preface to "An Order of Sunday Worship Using the Basic Pattern" in The United Methodist Book of Worship (page 16) states,

> While the freedom and diversity of United Methodist worship are greater than can be represented by any single order of worship, United Methodists also affirm a heritage of order and the importance of the specific guidance and modeling that an order of worship provides. . . . Acts of worship that reflect racial, ethnic, regional, and local customs and heritages may be used appropriately throughout this order.[11]

The ritual officially approved by The United Methodist Church represents the decisions of the church about the theology and practice of Holy Communion. This ritual expresses the unity of the universal church of Jesus Christ and exemplifies our connection within The United Methodist Church. It had its origin in the early Christian community and has evolved in the practice of the church through the centuries. Our ritual is in accord with those currently used in most Christian bodies.

At its best, United Methodist liturgy combines the order and beauty of established ritual with the vitality and freshness of creative expression. The richness of tradition developed through two thousand years of Christian history can be faithfully adapted for present times and situations.

## Practice:

Bishops, pastors, and congregations are expected to use the services of Word and Table in the official United Methodist hymnals and books of worship. Knowledgeable use of these resources allows for a balance of flexibility to meet contextual needs and order that reflects our unity and connectional accountability.

1. Discuss: How often does your congregation celebrate the Lord's Supper? Are there special occasions of offering the sacrament in addition to this regular schedule? Suggest some ways by which your congregation might be encouraged toward more frequent Eucharist. What objections might be raised and how would you answer them?

*2. Discuss the concept of "the priesthood of all believers." Examine "A Service of Word and Table I" (BOW, pages 33–39, and the Appendix in this study guide) and mention the points at which the congregation is actively involved. Describe an occasion on which you felt that you were truly a vital part of Eucharistic worship.

3. Discuss. Have you as a layperson ever been involved in preparing or serving Holy Communion? If so, how were you impacted by this role?

4. Construct on markerboard or newsprint an outline of the main parts of the Great Thanksgiving. Discuss: Why is each of these parts important?

5. Discuss: What gestures and postures are used by your pastor and congregation in celebrating the sacrament? Are these meaningful to your people?

6. Ask: Does your congregation extend the table by taking Holy Communion to those who cannot attend? Discuss ways to get more laypeople involved in this ministry. Say: If you have participated in this ministry, describe to the group your experience and how you felt about it.

7. Discuss: How closely does the usual service of Holy Communion in your church accord with the ritual in the Hymnal? What important aspects might be missing in the service if the ritual is not used?

Suggest some variations in the service that might be both meaningful and faithful.

*8. Ask group members to read in advance and be prepared to lead discussion on "The Role of Artists in Worship," by Sara Webb Phillips (pages 160–166), and "Using Media in Worship," by Thomas E. Boomershine (pages 167–172), in *Worship Matters: A United Methodist Guide to Ways to Worship, Volume 1* (Discipleship Resources).

## To Expand the Study
### *(for clergy and in academic settings)*

*1. Read John Wesley's sermon "The Duty of Constant Communion," (pages 65–70 of this study guide). Note the objections to frequent Communion that he mentions and how he answers them. How can this sermon be effectively used with your congregations?

2. What changes could be made in your worship services in order to facilitate moving to meaningful celebrations of weekly Holy Communion?

*3. Read in advance Chapter Six of Laurence Hull Stookey's *Eucharist: Christ's Feast With the Church* and utilize it in your discussion.

4. Discuss how in preaching and teaching you might lead your people to understand themselves as active participants in the Eucharist. (*Creative Preaching on the Sacraments*, by Craig A. Satterlee and Lester Ruth, might be helpful. Check especially pages 28–31, 34–38, and 44.)

5. Examine the words of the Great Thanksgiving, noting the theological concepts and biblical themes that comprise it.

6. Make copies (the publisher allows this for local church use) and study together

"An Order of Sunday Worship Using the Basic Pattern" (*UMH*; pages 3–5) offers flexibility for response to the activity of the Holy Spirit as well as the specifics of events and settings. In attending to the season, day, or occasion, presiders may insert words of their own composition or selections taken from fuller ritual texts as indicated in "A Service of Word and Table II" and "A Service of Word and Table III." (See *UMH*, "A Service of Word and Table II," pages 12–15; "A Service of Word and Table III," pages 15–16; and musical settings, pages 17–25.) Pastors using *Mil Voces Para Celebrar* or *Come, Let Us Worship* may apply these directions to the use of the respective rituals in those books. Material from different regions and cultures may also enrich our celebrations.

Pastors and congregations in ecumenical shared-ministry settings will necessarily need to incorporate and use the rituals of the denominations comprising those parishes in ways that are responsible and respectful, both of United Methodist understandings and practices and of those of the other traditions represented.

In accord with our commitments to the pursuit of Christian unity and seeking shared Communion, bishops, pastors, and congregations are encouraged to use the Word and Table ritual from other denominations. Such use is to be compatible with our Basic Pattern of Worship and with United Methodist liturgical and theological commitments.

## Endnotes

1 Copyright © 1992 by The United Methodist Publishing House.

2 From *Didache*, section 14, in *Early Christian Fathers*. Translation by Cyril C. Richardson.

3 From *First Apology*, Chapter 67, in *Early Christian Fathers*, edited by Cyril C. Richardson. Translation by Edward Rochie Hardy.

4 From "The Duty of Constant Communion."

5 From "Letter to Dr. Coke, Mr. Asbury, and Our Brethren in North America."

6 From "The Baptismal Covenant I," © 1976, 1980, 1985, 1989, 1992 UMPH.

7 From Services of Word and Table, © The United Methodist Publishing House.

8 From "A Service of Word and Table I," © 1972, 1980, 1985, 1989 The United Methodist Publishing House.

9 From "A Service of Word and Table V," © 1976, 1980 by Abingdon; © 1985, 1987, 1992 UMPH.

10 From "The Order for the Ordination of Elders," © 1979 by Board of Discipleship, The United Methodist Church.

11 From "An Order of Sunday Worship Using the Basic Pattern," © 1985, 1989, 1992 UMPH.

"Extending the Eucharist to the Unwillingly Absent," pages 155–159 in Laurence Hull Stookey's *Eucharist: Christ's Feast With the Church*. Design appropriate training and resources for laypeople who administer the consecrated elements to those unable to be present at corporate celebrations.

7. Discuss the consistent use of the Holy Communion ritual in the *Hymnal* (see "Practice," page 40 of this book). What are the values? Are there occasions when you might modify the ritual or use an alternative? When and why would you do this? (Examine the resources available in *The Book of Worship*, pages 16–32, as well as the section specifically related to "Services of Word and Table.")

## Endnotes

1 English translation of *Sursum Corda* prepared by the English Language Liturgical Consultation (ELLC), 1988.

2 From "'Do This.' Thoughts on the Reception and Implementation of *This Holy Mystery*," by Mark W. Stamm, O.S.L., in *Sacramental Life*, Fall 2004; pages 818–819.

## Servants at the Table

### Presiding Ministers: Elders and Licensed Local Pastors

#### Principle:

An ordained elder or a person authorized under the provisions of the *Book of Discipline* presides at all celebrations of Holy Communion.

#### Background:

In accord with the practice of the church throughout Christian history, God calls and the church sets apart certain people for leadership within the body of Christians. We believe that the Holy Spirit gives to such people the grace and gifts they need for leadership in obedience to their call. The meaning and purpose of ordination are described in ¶¶ 301–303 in the *Book of Discipline*.

Elders are ordained to a lifetime ministry of service, word, sacrament, and order (*BOD*; ¶ 332) and charged "to administer the sacraments of baptism and the Supper of the Lord according to Christ's ordinance" and "to encourage the private and congregational use of the other means of grace" (*BOD*; ¶ 340.2.*a* and *b*).

John Wesley drew a sharp distinction between the preaching ministry, which was open to lay men and women, and the priestly ministry of administering the sacraments, which was to be exercised only by those ordained as elders. Recounting the 1744 preachers' conference, Wesley wrote, "None of them dreamed, that the being called to preach gave them any right to administer sacraments. . . . 'You are to do that part of the work which we appoint.' But what work was this? Did we ever appoint you to administer sacraments; to exercise the priestly office? Such a design never entered into our mind; it was the farthest from our thoughts."[1] Wesley insisted that there could be no sacramental ministry without ordination as elder.

People participating in Eucharistic ministry include both clergy and laity. Within the clergy category, there are elders, licensed local pastors, and deacons. Changes in 1996 in the ordering of ministry in The United Methodist Church have raised new questions about the proper roles of each of these groups. Clearly, ordained elders are authorized to administer the sacraments at all times and places. The *Discipline* describes their ordination as being to service, word, sacrament, and order. Licensed local pastors are not ordained elders, although they may be in the process of working toward ordination. Since 1976, though, our denomination has authorized them to administer the sacraments in the places of ministry to which they are appointed by their bishop. This authorization is an exception to the requirement of elders' orders. It is accepted because licensed local pastors serve as pastors-in-charge in many congregations. Those congregations can best receive the sacraments regularly if their pastor is able to serve them. Indeed, in some cases people in these (usually small) churches might be denied the sacraments for long periods if their local licensed pastors were not able to baptize them and offer Holy Communion.

Deacons are also ordained clergy in our church. This category of ministry was established by the General Conference in 1996, and the church is still coming to understand it fully. Most people who were ordained as deacons prior to 1996 were ordained to a

transitional status. They went on to become elders when they had completed their ordination process. There are still people in this category today who have not yet completed the process (¶ 369), although their number is decreasing each year. Most deacons today, however, are ordained in full connection with their annual conferences. They have that status permanently; it is a separate order from elders. Deacons are ordained to word and service, but not to sacrament. This means that for the first time in our denomination's history, ordination and sacramental authority are separated. Deacons serve in a variety of significant ministries, but they are not expected to be pastors-in-charge of congregations. They assist elders in administering baptism and Holy Communion and should have distinct roles in these services. The question of sacramental authority and responsibility for ordained deacons is debated within United Methodism today. Some argue that deacons should be able to administer the sacraments in their appointed places of work if no elder is available. Others point out that deacons are to be in relationship with local congregations and that they can connect the church with the institutions in which they serve by taking the consecrated elements to people there. The discussion continues; but for the present, the *Discipline* is clear that deacons are not ordained to sacrament.

In accord with the tenet that the whole gathered community should be actively engaged in Eucharistic celebration, laypeople read Scripture and lead prayers (not the Great Thanksgiving), prepare the table and elements, bring the elements forward in offering, help distribute the consecrated elements to those communing, and render other appropriate service. Ordained leaders have the responsibility of recruiting and training people for these services. Confi-

This conviction ultimately determined his decision to perform "extra-ordinary" ordinations himself.

"The authority of the ordained minister," according to "Baptism, Eucharist and Ministry," "is rooted in Jesus Christ, who has received it from the Father (Matt. 28:18), and who confers it by the Holy Spirit through the act of ordination. This act takes place within a community which accords public recognition to a particular person."[2] Elders administer the sacraments as authorized representatives of the church.

Under the terms of the *Book of Discipline*, several groups of people are authorized to preside at Eucharist in the charges to which they are appointed. These include associate member deacons, deacons ordained under the provisions of the 1992 *Book of Discipline*, licensed local pastors, and commissioned ministers licensed for pastoral ministry (*BOD*; ¶¶ 339, 340, 315, 316). Some of these provisions have been in effect since 1976 in order to enable the sacraments to be served regularly in many small congregations that do not have elders as their pastors. The church continues to seek the best ways to meet this need and still uphold the historic linkage of ordination and administration of the sacraments.

### Practice:

Bishops and district superintendents are elders who are assigned and appointed to exercise the ministry of superintending (*BOD*; ¶¶ 403 and 404) as an expression of the connectional nature of The United Methodist Church. To embody the connectional nature of the church and its sacramental life, a bishop or district superintendent who is present may be invited to preside at Holy Communion.

An elder or a person authorized under the provisions of the *Book of Discipline* presides at all celebrations of Holy Communion. While some portions of the order of worship may be led by others, an elder or authorized pastor leads the congregation in praying the Great Thanksgiving, in which the whole assembly takes an active role. (See the Sanctus, the memorial acclamation, and the Amen, all printed in bold type, in *UMH*, pages 9–10.)

Elders who are in extension ministries and retired elders may be asked to preside when they are needed in local churches or on other sacramental occasions. "All conference members who are elders in full connection, including those in extension ministries, shall be available and on call to administer the sacraments of baptism and the Lord's Supper as required by the *Discipline* (¶ 340.2.a) and requested by the

This Holy Mystery

district superintendent of the district in which the appointment is held" (*BOD*; ¶ 344.3.*a*). Those in the Order of Elders are encouraged to make every effort to be available for presiding when Holy Communion is needed or desired.

All elders or deacons who are present may be invited to participate in leadership of the service, stand with the presider at the table, and assist in distributing the elements.

All who lead Holy Communion should be knowledgeable and prepared in Eucharistic theology, spirituality, and practice, including the roles of those assisting. This ministry is under the supervision of district superintendents and pastoral mentors (*BOD*; ¶ 316.4).

## Assisting Ministers: Deacons and Laity

### Principle:

Deacons are ordained to the ministry of word and service (*BOD*; ¶ 329) and charged to "give leadership in the Church's life" in, among other ways, "assisting the elders in the administration of the sacraments" and "in the congregation's mission to the world" (¶ 328).

### Background:

"Within the church community, there are persons whose gifts, evidence of God's grace, and promise of future usefulness are affirmed by the community, and who respond to God's call by offering themselves in leadership as ordained ministers" (*BOD*; ¶ 301.2). Deacons, as well as elders, are ordained to the ministry of leadership in The United Methodist Church.

This ordination of a deacon is to a life of linking the church's worship to Christ's service in the world. In worship it is appropriate for deacons to lead, or recruit and support others to lead, those parts of the liturgy that manifest the connection between our worship and Christian witness in daily life.

### Practice:

In continuity with historic and ecumenical practice ("Baptism, Eucharist and Ministry"), the role of deacon in services of Word and Table appropriately includes reading the Gospel lesson; leading the concerns and prayers for the world, the church, and the needy; receiving the elements and preparing the table before the Great Thanksgiving; assisting the elder in serving the Communion elements; setting the table in order; and dismissing the people to serve before the elder offers God's blessing. Further, deacons have a significant role in

dence, consistency, and effectiveness are essential in making this lay ministry meaningful to all in the congregation.

## Teaching and Learning

### Resources and Materials

- Copies of *The Book of Discipline—2004*
- Markerboard or newsprint and markers
- *Quarterly Review,* Winter 1999–2000
- *Worship Matters: A United Methodist Guide to Ways to Worship, Volume 1,* E. Byron Anderson, editor

1. Consider the roles of ordained clergy in the church. Why are such designated groups of people needed?

*2. Read "The Meaning of Ordination and Conference Membership" in the *Discipline* (¶¶ 301–304). Talk about how this material informs your understanding of ordained ministry.

*3. Read "The Ordained Elder in Full Connection" in the *Discipline* (¶¶ 332–336). List on a markerboard or newsprint the roles of the elder.

*4. Read "The Ordained Deacon in Full Connection" in the *Discipline* (¶¶ 328–331). List the roles of the deacon.

5. If your congregation is fortunate enough to have a deacon on staff, what roles does that person fill in your worship and sacramental services? How do these roles compare with the roles listed in "This Holy Mystery" (pages 45–46 of this book)?

6. Discuss as many ways as you can think of that laypeople can be involved in the Eucharistic ministry of the church. What kind of training do these people need to have?

## To Expand the Study

### *(for clergy and in academic settings)*

*1. Read in advance "Elders and Deacons: Renewed Orders and Partnership in Leading Worship," in *Quarterly Review*, Winter 1999–2000, pages 387–403. Read also two articles from *Worship Matters: A United Methodist Guide to Ways to Worship, Volume I*: "The Role of the Presider," by E. Byron Anderson, pages 123–129, and "The Role of Deacons and Assisting Ministers," by Daniel T. Benedict, Jr., and M. Anne Burnette Hook, pages 130–136.

2. Discuss Wesley's distinction between the preaching ministry and the priestly ministry ("Background," page 43 of this book). How might this understanding influence your own service?

3. How do you understand the ministry of deacons in full connection? Should they be empowered to consecrate the Eucharist in their places of service?

4. Discuss the 1976 compromise of allowing licensed local pastors and others who are not elders to administer the sacraments in congregations to which they are appointed. Are there other, perhaps better, solutions in these situations? What kinds of training in course of study or licensing schools do these leaders need?

preparing for the service by organizing, assembling the necessary elements and containers, and making assignments for other participants, including those taking the meal to those unable to attend. Deacons are designated to serve as links between the church and the world. Their ministry appropriately includes taking the consecrated elements from their congregations and serving them in their places of ministry.

Deacons need training and preparation for their diverse roles in Eucharistic ministry.

### Principle:

All members of Christ's universal church are, through their baptism, called to share in the Eucharistic ministry that is committed to the whole church (*BOD*; ¶ 220). Lay people assist the presider in leading the whole congregation to celebrate the Lord's Supper.

### Background:

In the section titled "The Ministry of All Christians," *The Book of Discipline* says, "All Christians are called through their baptism to this ministry of servanthood in the world to the glory of God and for human fulfillment" (¶ 125).

In depicting the church as a body of many parts, Paul declares in 1 Corinthians 12:7: "To each is given the manifestation of the Spirit for the common good." This diversity of ministry requires cooperation within the body of Christ, since it is only through such cooperation that the body is complete (1 Corinthians 12:12-31). It is important for liturgical celebrations to embody the active participation of all those gathered, as a demonstration of the full ministry of the body of Christ in the world.

As each layperson fulfills his or her vital ministry in worship, some will be called to exercise various leadership roles. "The United Methodist tradition has recognized that laypersons as well as ordained persons are gifted and called by God to lead the Church. The servant leadership of these persons is essential to the mission and ministry of congregations" (*BOD*; ¶ 132). The whole of Part III of the *Book of Discipline* elaborates on this idea.

### Practice:

Pastors and other leaders facilitate the full and active engagement of the ministry of all laity in celebrations of Holy Communion. As part of this general liturgical ministry of all Christians, laypeople exercise leadership of worship by reading Scripture, leading prayers, preparing the table, providing and preparing the elements, distributing the elements, and helping with other parts of the service.

At the appropriate point in the service, laity representing the whole congregation may bring the elements forward to the Table as a part of the offering. The entire congregation responds in unison as indicated throughout the ritual. Laypeople may take the consecrated elements to members who are unable to attend the congregational celebration.

Laypeople need instruction and training for this leadership, under the supervision of pastors and deacons.

## Endnotes

1 From "The Ministerial Office," 11.
2 From "Baptism, Eucharist and Ministry," © 1982 WCC Publications, World Council of Churches, PO Box 2100, 1211 Geneva 2, Geneva, Switzerland; page 22.

# Setting the Table

## Setting the Table

### The Holy Communion Table

#### Principle:

The people and leaders gather around the elements for Holy Communion. The place where the elements are set is the Holy Communion table.

#### Background:

In the Old Testament, sacrifice was offered on an altar. In the Gospel narratives of the Last Supper, Jesus "took his place at the table, and the apostles with him" (Luke 22:14). Through time, the church increasingly understood the Eucharist as a repetition of Christ's sacrifice on the cross, and the Table came to be seen as an altar of sacrifice. It was moved against the wall of the sanctuary, and priests stood before the altar, with their backs to the congregation, to offer sacrifice to God.

The more radical Protestant reformers abandoned altars, preferring simple tables and reenactment of the Last Supper of Jesus with his disciples. Others, including the Church of England, of which John Wesley was a priest, retained the altar against a wall.

A twentieth-century international liturgical renewal movement, expressed in the changes of the Second Vatican Council of the Roman Catholic Church, made major reforms in worship. These reforms included moving the table into an open space so that the priest could stand behind it, giving the assembly a sense of meeting around it. The United Methodist Church, along with many other mainline churches, adopted revised rituals that call for the presiding minister to stand behind the Lord's Table, facing the people, from the offertory through the breaking of the bread (*BOW*, page 36).

The architecture and arrangement of our worship spaces are important because they communicate nonverbal messages to worshipers. For Holy Communion to be appreciated as a community meal with Christ, the table that holds the elements is significant. The table should be freestanding, about thirty-nine inches high, and situated so as to allow the presiding pastor to stand behind it facing the people. It should not be cluttered with other paraphernalia that might distract from the elements. It is preferable that the table not be referred to as the "altar," since that term carries the meaning of sacrifice and may obscure other rich meanings of the sacrament.

The design and arrangement of space for worship speaks a loud message about the relationship between God and the people and what is important in our worship experience. Many of our churches were built or renovated in a time when Holy Communion was infrequently celebrated and insufficiently appreciated. Even churches built or renovated in recent years have sometimes been designed without appropriate attention to the fullness of liturgical experience. When the unintended message of the architectural design contradicts our understanding of worship as encompassing the fullness of Word and Table, the message of the space will win. The design and use of space is a theological statement and needs to communicate authentically what we believe about the place of sacraments and sermons.

Session Six: Setting the Table    49

In the predecessor denominations of United Methodism, the consecrated elements were distributed and received in a variety of ways, including passing the elements through the pews, and the people coming forward to the altar or railing or serving stations. Consistent with our emphasis on the gift of grace, it is appropriate for the bread to be placed in the hands of the communicants rather than being taken by them. Rising and moving forward to receive seems to best exemplify our belief in the necessity of human response to divine grace. It has been common practice for people to kneel to receive and then to be dismissed by table groups. In the last half century, intinction has become widely used. In this mode, people come forward to receive the bread and dip it in the cup while standing. This method helps to answer complaints about the length of Eucharistic services, especially if multiple serving stations are offered. Opportunity for communicants to kneel in prayer before returning to their seats, though, is important to many.

The bread used in Holy Communion is a sign of the body of Christ offered for our redemption and a sign of the church constituted as the body of Christ. While necessary variations in its content and form are allowable, the bread should always communicate these meanings as clearly as possible. Use of a whole loaf, which is broken and distributed to those communing, illustrates the unity of the church. William McElvaney expresses this powerfully: "The common loaf evokes the hidden reality that we are a single fabric of hurting and hoping humanity."[1]

If other forms of bread must be used, care should be taken that they exemplify the abundant love of God. Tiny servings of cubes or wafers may not express divine generosity effectively. Prepackaged juice and

In a church building, the place where the elements are set is sometimes called the altar, but the terms *altar-table* and *Lord's Table* are preferable.

The rail that in some churches is located between the congregation and the chancel area, while not properly called the altar, is a sacred area for kneeling to receive Communion. People may also come to one or more stations where the elements are served and receive them standing, with an option of kneeling at the rail for prayer.

### *Practice:*

In our churches, the Communion table is to be placed in such a way that the presider is able to stand behind it, facing the people, and the people can visually if not physically gather around it. The table should be high enough so that the presider does not need to stoop to handle the bread and cup. Adaptations may be necessary to facilitate gracious leadership.

While architectural integrity should be respected, it is important for churches to carefully adapt or renovate their worship spaces more fully to invite the people to participate in the Holy Meal. If "altars" are for all practical purposes immovable, then congregations should make provisions for creating a table suitable to the space so that the presiding minister may face the people and be closer to them.

## The Communion Elements

### *Principle:*

In accordance with the words of Christ and Christian tradition, the church uses bread in celebrations of Holy Communion.

### *Background:*

Bread is used in both the Old and New Testaments to signify God's sustenance of human beings and the importance of our eating together. When God liberated the Hebrew people from slavery in Egypt, they carried their bread with them. The Jews have celebrated this exodus throughout the centuries as Passover. The provision of manna and the showbread (bread of the Presence) kept in the Tabernacle are examples of God's sustenance from the time of Israel's wandering in the wilderness (Exodus 16; 25:23-30). In the New Testament, Jesus shared meals frequently with his disciples and with others (Matthew 9:9-11 and similar passages). He fed the multitudes (Matthew 14:13-21 and parallels) and used bread to signify his identity and mission (John 6). On the eve of his crucifixion, Jesus ate the Last Supper with his disciples (Matthew 26:26-29 and parallels). After his resurrection, he broke bread with the travelers to Emmaus (Luke 24:13-35) and with his disciples on the seashore (John 21:9-14).

### Practice:

It is appropriate that the bread eaten in Holy Communion both look and taste like bread. The use of a whole loaf best signifies the unity of the church as the body of Christ and, when it is broken and shared, our fellowship in that body (1 Corinthians 10:16-17).

Historical continuity with the practice of the universal church is important; however, worship planners should be sensitive to local situations. Bread may be made from any grain according to availability. In ecumenical and other settings, wafers may be an appropriate choice.

The loaf should be plain bread (no frostings, nuts, raisins, artificial coloring, or other additions). Leavened or unleavened bread is equally acceptable. In congregations where there are people with gluten allergies, gluten-free bread may be offered. The loaf broken at the table is to be the bread distributed to the people. As appropriate to the dignity of the occasion, care should be taken to avoid excessive crumbling of the bread and to remove large pieces that fall to the floor.

### Principle:

In accordance with Scripture and Christian tradition, the historic and ecumenical church uses wine in celebrations of Holy Communion.

### Background:

Throughout the Old Testament story of God's relationship with the Hebrew people, blood was the sign of covenant ratification (Exodus 12:12-28; 24:1-8). At his last meal with the disciples, Jesus spoke of the wine as his blood— the blood of the new covenant (Jeremiah 31:31-34) between God and God's people, made possible through Christ's death and resurrection (Revelation 5:9). Jesus also spoke of the wine as a sign of the heavenly banquet that he will celebrate with the church in the future (1 Corinthians 11:23-26; Matthew 26:26-29).

The juice of the red grape in a common cup represents the church's covenant with Christ, established through his atoning death (Hebrews 9:15-28; 13:20-21), and fulfills Christ's commands at the Last Supper (Matthew 26:27-29; Mark 14:23-24; Luke 22:19-20).

Roman Catholicism, Eastern Orthodoxy, and many Protestant denominations have always used wine in the Eucharist. During the movement against beverage alcohol in the late nineteenth century, the predecessor bodies of The United Methodist Church turned to the use

wafer combinations are not appropriate in most circumstances. Bread torn from a common loaf should be in large enough pieces to evoke some sense of actual eating.

In contrast to the practice of historic and ecumenical Christianity, The United Methodist Church customarily uses unfermented grape juice in the Eucharist. This practice is the outcome of the temperance and prohibition movements of the late nineteenth and early twentieth centuries rather than theological principle. Unfermented juice was not easily attainable until Dr. Thomas Welch of New Jersey successfully applied to grape juice the pasteurization process first developed for milk. Differences of opinion on this matter today reflect continuing tension in United Methodism between the Catholic-Anglican and the evangelical-free church aspects of our heritage.

Use of a single cup or chalice for drinking or intinction (dipping pieces of bread into the cup) expresses the unity of the church. Some contemporary theological positions consider blood imagery to convey an undesirable view of the divine act of atonement. It is difficult, however, to grasp the biblical understanding of Christ's death against the backdrop of Old Testament covenantal theology without acknowledging the role of blood. Blood may be understood as more than the atonement of the Old Testament, though. Blood is a symbol of Christ's offering of life, given as a new covenant to live in and through us as a sign of our participation in "the divine nature." The symbolism of Christ's blood of the new covenant is clearest when red or purple juice is served.

People who have allergies or other conditions that make consumption of the bread or juice/wine problematic need to be assured that their Communion is complete if they receive

only one of the elements. In situations of illness the server may simply touch a person's mouth with the bread dipped in the cup.

Disposal of the consecrated elements that are left over after all have been served is a significant theological action. These elements are no longer physical bread and juice only; they have been set apart for holy use. They are to be used to take the sacrament to those unable to attend. If there is more than is needed for that purpose, clergy and laity may reverently consume the extra after the service or dispose of them by returning them to the earth.

Care should be taken in the preparation and serving of the elements to protect their cleanliness. In our concern about communicable diseases, actions within the service may reassure congregations that hygiene is being considered. Preparation can include servers washing their hands with water and antibacterial soap just prior to the Great Thanksgiving. It is more sanitary—as well as more theologically appropriate—for servers to place a piece of bread into the hands of the people, rather than for people to tear bread from the loaf or take it from a plate. Cups made of metals such as gold and silver inhibit bacteria while glass and ceramic cups do not have this property. If individual cups must be used to satisfy hygienic concerns, they can be filled from a single pouring cup as part of the service. Reusable cups should be thoroughly washed and dried in a manner consistent with the highest possible standards of hygiene available. Disposable individual cups may be preferred.

## Teaching and Learning

### Resources and Materials

• *Sunday Dinner: The Lord's Supper and the Christian Life*, by William H. Willimon

of unfermented grape juice. This continues to be the position of the denomination. (The term *wine* is used in this document because of its biblical and historical antecedents, although United Methodists customarily serve unfermented grape juice in Holy Communion.)

The use of a common cup dates back to the Last Supper where Jesus takes a single cup of wine, blesses it, and gives it to the disciples. It is a powerful symbol of the unity of the body of Christ gathered at the Lord's Table.

### Practice:

Variations may be necessary in cultural contexts where the juice of the grape is unavailable or prohibitively expensive.

A single cup or chalice may be used for intinction—dipping the bread into the wine—or for drinking. The use of a common chalice best represents Christian unity, but individual cups are used in many congregations. In these situations, unity can be effectively symbolized if each person's cup is filled from a pouring chalice.

⁓

### Principle:

The consecrated elements are to be treated with reverent respect and appreciation as gifts of God's creation that have, in the words of the Great Thanksgiving, become "for us the body and blood of Christ"[1] (*UMH*; page 10).

### Background:

We do not worship the consecrated elements nor reserve them for adoration. We respect the elements because God is using them for holy purposes—reconstituting the assembly as the body of Christ, conveying grace, forgiving sin, foreshadowing heaven, and strengthening the faithful for the journey of salvation. Although they have undergone no substantive (physical) change, the elements have been consecrated—set apart for sacred use.

While, in the history of the church, reverence for the consecrated elements has sometimes led to superstition, proper respect for the elements helps Christians grow in authentic sacramental piety.

As Article XVIII of The Articles of Religion of the Methodist Church makes clear, United Methodism rejects any suggestion that the bread and wine used in Communion are transformed or transubstantiated into other substances:

Transubstantiation, or the change of the substance of bread and wine in the Supper of our Lord, cannot be proved by Holy Writ, but is repugnant to the plain words of Scripture, overthroweth the nature of a sacrament, and hath given occasion to many superstitions.

The body of Christ is given, taken, and eaten in the Supper, only after a heavenly and spiritual manner. And the mean whereby the body of Christ is received and eaten in the Supper is faith.

*(BOD; page 64)*

(The United Methodist Church notes that the anti-Roman Catholic tone of Article XVIII reflects the "bitterly polemical" relationships of past centuries and "rejoice[s] in the positive contemporary relationships that are being developed . . . at levels both official and unofficial" [*BOR*; pages 272–273].)

*The Book of Worship* directs, "What is done with the remaining bread and wine should express our stewardship of God's gifts and our respect for the holy purpose they have served"[2] (page 30).

### Practice:

The practice of consecrating elements ahead of time for the convenience of the pastor not having to go to small or remote congregations, weekend camps, or other such occasions is inappropriate and contrary to our historic doctrine and understanding of how God's grace is made available in the sacrament (Article XVIII, The Articles of Religion, *BOD*; page 64). If authorized leadership is not available for celebrating the Lord's Supper, other worship services such as love feasts, agape meals, or baptismal reaffirmations are valid alternatives that avoid the misuse of Communion elements.

The consecrated elements of bread and wine are used for distribution to the sick and others who wish to commune but are unable to attend congregational worship. If any bread and wine remain, they should always be disposed of by (1) the pastor and/or others at the pastor's direction consuming them in a reverent manner following the service; (2) returning them to the earth by pouring (2 Samuel 23:16), burying, scattering, or burning.

## Hygiene and Table Setting

### Principle:

Those who prepare the elements and give them to the people are to demonstrate care that the bread and cup are administered so as to minimize contamination.

### Background:

In administering the elements to the people, both perception and reality of hygiene are important. The people have justifiable health

• Bibles
• Markerboard or newsprint and markers
• *American Methodist Worship*, by Karen B. Westerfield Tucker

*1. Ask the group to read in advance "Let's Get Together," pages 102–110 in *Sunday Dinner: The Lord's Supper and the Christian Life*, by William H. Willimon. Discuss this material together.

2. Describe the arrangements of and around the Communion table in your congregation. Are there ways that these arrangements could be changed in order to enhance services of Holy Communion?

3. What kinds or forms of bread have you seen served in the Lord's Supper? What do you think communicates most powerfully the meaning of the sacrament?

4. Read Exodus 16 and 25:23-30 for examples of the significance of bread in the Old Testament. Read John 6 and note how Jesus used bread in speaking about himself.

5. Read 1 Corinthians 10:16-17 and discuss its significance for fellowship and unity in the community of faith.

6. List on a markerboard or newsprint the arguments for and against the use of wine rather than or in addition to grape juice in Holy Communion.

7. Explain how the United Methodist practice of treating the consecrated elements with respect differs from Roman Catholic understandings and practice.

8. How big an issue in your congregation is hygienic practice in the Eucharist? How helpful is handwashing by the presiding pastor just prior to touching the bread? Are there other practices that might be instituted to allay health concerns?

## To Expand the Study
### (for clergy and in academic settings)

1. Discuss the nonverbal messages that are conveyed to congregations by the position and posture of the presiding minister.

*2. Read in advance then discuss "The Elements for Communion and the Method of Reception," pages 150–154 in Karen B. Westerfield Tucker's *American Methodist Worship*.

3. Discuss this quotation from William H. Willimon, *Sunday Dinner: The Lord's Supper and the Christian Life*, page 70: "Communion bread should be placed in someone's hand by the server, looking into the person's eyes, calling the person's Christian (first) name if possible: 'Jane, the Body of Christ, given for you.' This moment should be total, personal, and sensitively done."[2]

## Endnotes

1 From *Eating and Drinking at the Welcome Table: The Holy Supper for All People*, by William K. McElvaney (The Chalice Press, 1998); page 23.

2 *Sunday Dinner: The Lord's Supper and the Christian Life*, by William H. Willimon, © 1981 The Upper Room.

concerns that the signs of the body and blood of Christ given to them at the Holy Meal are handled carefully and with concern for hygiene.

This need for care and hygiene should be considered along with scientific studies that make it clear that those who partake in Holy Communion have no higher incidence of illness than those who do not.

Concern and planning are necessary in situations of serious illness and for accommodating at the Table those whose immune systems are compromised. The counsel of Romans 14 and 15 can guide our practice.

### Practice:

Those who will prepare and serve the elements should wash their hands. This can be done simply and without creating an additional layer of ceremony in the service.

The piece of bread given should be sizeable enough to be a generous sign and to be able to be dipped in the cup without the fingers of the recipient dipping into the liquid.

## Endnotes

1 From "A Service of Word and Table I," © 1972, 1980, 1985, 1989 The United Methodist Publishing House.

2 From "An Order of Sunday Worship Using the Basic Pattern," © 1985, 1989, 1992 UMPH.

## Extending the Table

### Holy Communion and Evangelism

#### *Principle:*

The Lord's Supper forms the church into a community of evangelism that reaches out to preach, teach, baptize, and make new disciples of Christ (Matthew 28:19-20).

#### *Background:*

Immediately after his account of the institution of the Lord's Supper in 1 Corinthians 11–12, Paul moves into an extended discussion of the body of Christ composed of many members whose gifts for ministry are diverse. Paul understood the sacrament of Holy Communion to form and shape the church for its mission of redeeming the world. In 2 Corinthians 5:16–6:10, he describes more fully "the ministry of reconciliation" that is the work of the church as "ambassadors for Christ."

United Methodists have inherited a tradition that emphasizes that spiritual benefits are not received for ourselves alone but also to prepare and propel us for the work of evangelism. In our prayer after Communion, we give thanks for what we have received and ask God to "grant that we may go into the world in the strength of your Spirit, to give ourselves for others"[1] (*UMH*; page 11).

*The Book of Discipline* emphasizes the imperative of evangelism: "The people of God, who are the church made visible in the world, must convince the world of the reality of the gospel or leave it unconvinced. There can be no evasion or delegation of this responsibility; the church is either faithful as a witnessing and serving community, or it loses its vitality and its impact on an unbelieving world" (¶ 128).

The significance of Holy Communion is not limited to the participating congregation or to the occasion of the sacramental celebration. Encounter with the living Christ at the Table transforms people and empowers them for the ministry of evangelism. The church must never be content simply to enjoy fellowship with those familiar people who share the Table. It must engage in the active work of outreach—proclaiming the gospel, bringing sinners to repentance, welcoming those who respond to the good news, and incorporating them into the community of faith.

Sacramentalism and evangelism have sometimes been considered in opposition to each other. This idea is a distortion of the gospel message and, particularly, of the teaching and practice of John Wesley. Participation in the sacraments is one of the most potent ways by which people are imbued with the imperative to engage in evangelism. The sacraments are not chiefly ends in themselves; they are means to enable the church to continue Christ's ministry of redeeming the world. Because all are valued and loved by God, this is a ministry that should reach out to all people, especially those who are oppressed, discriminated against, and rejected. There is an African-American spiritual entitled "I'm Gonna Eat at the Welcome Table." It includes the line, "Here all the world will find a welcome." Pastors and congregations should intentionally and repeatedly ask themselves who is absent from the Table in their celebrations. What groups of people are

being neglected? Are we sending messages of rejection to some? Is this congregation inclusive of all races and cultures, all economic and social strata, all sexual identities and forms of family? Are any of these outside the love of God and the need for divine grace?

Just as the Wesleyan revival was sacramental, specifically Eucharistic, so spiritual revival in the church today can be kindled and sustained through Holy Communion. The grace received in the Lord's Supper is a "grace unto." It is grace unto forgiveness, new life, and sanctification. At every point of our journeys of salvation, the Eucharist offers the grace we need—to repent, to be healed and forgiven, to trust, to be transformed, to be reconciled, to resist sin, to continue to grow ever more perfectly into the image of Christ, to recognize ourselves as the body of Christ in and for the world. There should be a direct linkage between our partaking of Holy Communion and our living lives of committed Christian discipleship.

> "Meeting with the risen Lord at the heart of worship must never be a dead end! It is a turnabout, a transformation point for the outward journey into a needy and hurting world. Home is not only where you go for rest, belonging, and nourishment; it is where identity and mission are formed and from which we go to serve."[1]

Holiness involves our personal ethical decisions and actions. Holiness also involves our work for justice and peace in the world. William McElvaney issues a powerful call that might be heard as an indictment:

> When we eat and drink at the welcome table, pertinent questions call our names and demand to be heard. The lesions of humanity are legion and are forever connected by this sacrament with origins of liberation.

### Practice:

Through the grace received in continual participation in the Lord's Supper, the community of faith reaches beyond itself to proclaim and exemplify the good news of salvation in Jesus Christ.

In Christian education and congregational life, we teach about the significance and meaning of the sacraments so that the faithful appreciate their own spiritual journey and are empowered to be knowledgeable and hospitable guides to those who seek Christ.

As members of the congregation partake of the Lord's Supper, the bonds of love within are strengthened and the worshiping community is empowered to reach out in dynamic and meaningful ways to evangelize and to work for peace and justice.

### Principle:

As followers of Jesus, who ate with sinners and reached out to the marginalized, the church must intentionally concern itself about those who are absent from Christ's Table—those who feel unworthy, the poor, the unconverted, victims of prejudice, and others who are oppressed or neglected.

### Background:

One of the themes of the Gospels, most prominent in Luke, is Jesus' ongoing efforts to teach the disciples that God's love and favor are extended to all people, not just those of a certain ethnicity, status, economic or political standing, or gender. The Book of Acts records some of the attempts of the early Christian community to define its limits, and God's continued efforts to broaden its inclusiveness. Peter's vision in Acts 10 is a particularly dramatic example.

Early English Methodists were typically (with some notable exceptions) from the socioeconomic groups that we might today speak of as the working poor. Wesley realized that a community of people who lived according to his General Rules (BOD; pages 71–74) were inevitably going to rise in status. He preached fervently against the dangers of money and the spiritual weakness that often accompanies prosperity.

In "The Ministry of All Christians," The Book of Discipline asserts: "We are called to be faithful to the example of Jesus' ministry to all persons. Inclusiveness means openness, acceptance, and support that enables all persons to participate in the life of the Church, the community, and the world. Thus, inclusiveness denies every semblance of discrimination" (¶ 138).

*Practice:*

The church is to consciously identify and seek out those who feel unwelcome, even excluded, from its congregations and to invite them to become part of the body of Christ and join in its celebrations of Holy Communion.

## Holy Communion and Ethical Christian Discipleship

*Principle:*

The sacraments are God's gifts to the gathered body of believers to form the church into Christ's body in ministry to the world. Through Holy Communion, the Holy Spirit works to shape our moral and ethical lives. In the ongoing process of conversion, we grow in personal and social holiness and are empowered to work for healing, compassion, reconciliation, justice, and peace.

*Background:*

The Old Testament prophets denounced the injustice and oppression that they saw around them. They proclaimed a God who acts in favor of the poor and powerless and calls God's people so to act. (Isaiah 1:16-17; 58:6-9; Amos 2:6-8; 5:11-15, 21-24; and Micah 6:6-8 are among a multitude of such passages.) When Jesus began his public ministry, he announced his mission:

> The Spirit of the Lord is upon me,
> because he has anointed me to bring good news to the poor.
> He has sent me to proclaim release to the captives
> and recovery of sight to the blind,
> to let the oppressed go free,
> to proclaim the year of the Lord's favor.
>
> (Luke 4:18-21)

He associated with those who were stigmatized and despised. Much of his teaching addressed economic and social inequality. Following his example, the early Christian community tried to care for the needs of all people (Acts 4:32-35; James 1:27; 2:14-17).

The United Methodist Church has a heritage from John Wesley in which ethical discipleship was inextricably related to sacramental worship. From concern by the Holy Club for the imprisoned, through care of the sick by the societies, to Wesley's own lifelong giving away of most of his money, the early Wesleyan movement sought to ease the suffering of the needy. Wesley made the linkage explicit when he wrote, "The Gospel of Christ knows of no religion, but social; no holiness but social holiness."[2] Collection at the Lord's Supper of alms to be given to the poor is a historic practice that many congregations in our tradition continue.

What does it mean to offer and receive the body of Christ when multitudes of our neighbors in the world are starving? Or the blood of Christ poured for you and me when so much blood is shed daily on our streets of violence? What are the implications of visually and viscerally remembering the Prince of Peace in a nuclear age? What kind of difference might it make to receive the Lord's Supper, a meal related to the Passover tradition, in view of the Holocaust and the long history of anti-Semitic elements in Christian theology and practice? In a world unsafe for women, and all too often in the church as well, does the eucharist make a difference?

What can it mean that we ingest the bread and wine at the table or altar next to one who just this week was presented a diagnosis of multiple myeloma? Or experienced the loss of a child? Or the loss of a job due to corporate downsizing? Obviously these are huge and difficult questions, but we dare not extend our hearts and hands to receive the bread and wine of Jesus Christ as though the church existed solely for the benefit of its own members.[2]

The sacrament of Holy Communion is God's gift to the entire Christian church. As United Methodists, we understand that we are only one small part of that greater body of Christ. Participating in Eucharist reminds us of both our unity with all Christians and the divisions within the church. United Methodists join in the Eucharistic celebrations of other Christians when we are welcome to do so. We invite all baptized Christians to commune with us when they are present at our celebrations. Our church has been in the past and is now involved in bilateral dialogues with

other denominations—the Evangelical Lutheran Church of America and the Episcopal Church, for examples—in the hope of establishing full communion. We are also working with Churches Uniting in Christ toward similar goals. United Methodists enter into these discussions with faithfulness to our own tradition and sources of authority and with respect for those of other groups.

## Teaching and Learning

### Resources and Materials

• Bibles
• Markerboard or newsprint and markers
• Copies of *The Book of Discipline—2004*
• "Baptism, Eucharist and Ministry"
• *Sacraments as God's Self-Giving Sacramental Practice and Faith*, by James F. White
• *The Meaning of Holy Communion in The United Methodist Church*, by E. Byron Anderson

1. Read 2 Corinthians 5:16–6:10 and talk about the evangelistic task of the church.

2. Discuss the meaning of the following phrase from the prayer after Communion: "Grant that we may go into the world in the strength of your Spirit, to give ourselves for others."[3] List on markerboard or newsprint specific actions that fulfilling this prayer might involve.

3. What is meant by sacramentalism? evangelism? Why are these two aspects of the faith sometimes considered to be in opposition?

4. Discuss and make a list of categories of people who are absent from the Communion Table in your congregation. How can you work to bring them in? Why must you do so?

By the early twentieth century, Methodists had begun to realize that holy living meant even more than acts of charity. Beginning with the Social Creed, American Methodists started to point out injustices caused by economic, social, and political structures and to call for the reform of such structures. The Social Principles in *The Book of Discipline* and the General Conference positions recorded in *The Book of Resolutions* show ongoing response to these concerns.

In carrying out our mission to make disciples of Jesus Christ, *The Book of Discipline* stipulates that the church is to "send persons into the world to live lovingly and justly as servants of Christ by healing the sick, feeding the hungry, caring for the stranger, freeing the oppressed, being and becoming a compassionate, caring presence, and working to develop social structures that are consistent with the gospel" (¶ 122).

Those who partake of Holy Communion are sent from the Table to be in ministry as Christ's presence in the world. God's people are sent to work compassionately for healing, reconciliation, justice, and peace. Such work requires prophetic, subversive actions: "renounc[ing] the spiritual forces of wickedness, reject[ing] the evil powers of this world, . . . accept[ing] the freedom and power God gives . . . to resist evil, injustice, and oppression in whatever forms they present themselves,"[3] (*BOW*; page 88) claiming and making real the victory of the risen Christ over all evil, sin, and death. Such faithful living in the power of the Holy Spirit answers the prayer in the Great Thanksgiving "that we may be for the world the body of Christ" and the petition "your kingdom come, your will be done" in the Lord's Prayer[4] (*UMH*; page 10). Celebrations of Holy Communion are, therefore, a foretaste of the realm of God, when God's future breaks into our present world. Here the church enacts the words of Jesus, "Then people will come from east and west, from north and south, and will eat in the kingdom of God" (Luke 13:29).

### Practice:

Holy Communion is to be conducted in ways that make apparent the inherent link between the Table and holy living, both individual and corporate. Participation in the Eucharist bears fruit in the world in attitudes and actions of personal and social holiness.

Communing with others in our congregations is a sign of community and mutual love between Christians throughout the church universal. The church must offer to the world a model of genuine community grounded in God's deep love for every person. As we eat and drink, we are motivated to act compassionately for those whose physical, emotional, and spiritual needs are unmet.

Receiving the bread and wine as products of divine creation reminds us of our duties of stewardship of the natural environment in a time when destruction and pollution imperil the earth and unjust distribution of the planet's resources destroys the hopes and lives of millions.

As we gratefully receive God's abundant grace, we are challenged to accept fully our responsibility and accountability for renewal of the social order, liberation for the oppressed, and the coming of the realm of God.

## Holy Communion and the Unity of the Church

### Principle:

Holy Communion expresses our oneness in the body of Christ, anticipates Jesus' invitation to feast at the heavenly banquet, and calls us to strive for the visible unity of the church.

### Background:

In its Constitution, The United Methodist Church affirms its ecumenical commitment:

> As part of the church universal, The United Methodist Church believes that the Lord of the church is calling Christians everywhere to strive toward unity; and therefore it will seek, and work for, unity at all levels of church life. (BOD; ¶ 6)

In "Our Doctrinal Heritage" in the Book of Discipline, the church affirms:

> United Methodists share a common heritage with Christians of every age and nation. This heritage is grounded in the apostolic witness to Jesus Christ as Savior and Lord, which is the source and measure of all valid Christian teaching. . . .
>
> With Christians of other communions we confess belief in the triune God—Father, Son, and Holy Spirit. This confession embraces the biblical witness to God's activity in creation, encompasses God's gracious self-involvement in the dramas of history, and anticipates the consummation of God's reign. (pages 41–43)

In the quest for greater visible unity, United Methodism has undertaken numerous concrete actions that express its commitment and promote ecumenical sharing:

1. Since the 1960's, the church has been involved with partners through Churches Uniting in Christ, formerly called the Consultation on Church Union. Throughout most of that history United Methodists have joined the partner churches in Holy Communion using

5. Read Isaiah 1:16-17 and 58:6-9, Amos 2:6-8 and 5:11-15, and Micah 6:6-8. Talk about what these passages say about the work of those who follow the divine will as a living expression of our communion with the triune God.

6. Discuss the meaning of John Wesley's words, "The Gospel of Christ knows of no religion, but social; no holiness but social holiness."[4]

7. Read aloud "Our Social Creed" (found at the end of the Social Principles in the Discipline, ¶ 166). Analyze the meaning of each of its paragraphs.

*8. In preparation for this session, find out as much as you can about the various dialogues that are taking place between United Methodism and other Christian bodies. You can get help from the General Commission on Christian Unity and Interreligious Concerns (gccuic.org).

9. Have you experienced fellowship and unity in the community of faith around the Table? Have you ever invited someone outside your church to participate with you in Holy Communion? Have you ever participated in the Lord's Supper in another church or denomination? How has this changed your way of viewing the sacrament?

10. Explore pages 10–17 of the ecumenical statement "Baptism, Eucharist and Ministry." List on markerboard or newsprint the points in the statement with which you agree and points with which you disagree. What aspects of Holy Communion are not addressed in this statement?

## To Expand the Study
### (for clergy and in academic settings)

*1. Read in advance "Sacraments and Justice," pages 93–113 in James F. White's

*Sacraments as God's Self-Giving: Sacramental Practice and Faith.* Discuss how your congregations do or do not understand the connections between Eucharistic celebration and working for peace and justice. How can you enable them to grasp and to live these connections?

2. Discuss Wesley's understanding of social holiness and its place in the journey of salvation. Consult the "Wesleyan Way or Order of Salvation," in the Appendix of this study guide, and "The Nature, Design, and General Rules of Our United Societies," on pages 72–74 of the *Discipline*.

3. E. Byron Anderson's *The Meaning of Holy Communion in The United Methodist Church* is a small booklet available inexpensively in packs of ten. Plan how you might use this resource in conjunction with leading the sessions of this study of "This Holy Mystery" in your congregation.

## Endnotes

1  From "This Holy Mystery: Planning for Holy Communion Throughout the Year—Part I," by Daniel Benedict, on www.umcworship.org; © 2004 The General Board of Discipleship of The United Methodist Church.

2  From *Eating and Drinking at the Welcome Table: The Holy Supper for All People*, by William K. McElvaney (The Chalice Press, 1998); page xiii.

3  From "A Service of Word and Table I," © 1972, 1980, 1985, 1989 The United Methodist Publishing House.

4  From *Preface to Hymns and Sacred Poems*.

liturgy approved by those churches for celebration together.

2. United Methodists across the world have entered into ecumenical agreements enhancing the unity of the church through recognition and reconciliation of ministries and sacraments.

3. Ecumenical representatives have been invited and encouraged to participate in United Methodist services of Holy Communion.

4. United Methodists have participated in the Eucharist services of other traditions when invited to do so, as an affirmation and reflection of our commitment to the church universal.

"Baptism, Eucharist and Ministry" affirms the significance of the sacrament for all Christians:

> It is in the eucharist that the community of God's people is fully manifested. Eucharistic celebrations always have to do with the whole Church, and the whole Church is involved in each local eucharistic celebration. In so far as a church claims to be a manifestation of the whole Church, it will take care to order its own life in ways which take seriously the interests and concerns of other churches.[5]

For churches such as the Orthodox and Roman Catholic, sharing the Eucharist between churches that are not in full agreement with one another is unacceptable because the Eucharist is itself a sign that unity and full agreement have been achieved. For other churches, including The United Methodist Church, the Eucharist can be a means to express the unity in Christ that already exists as a gift from God in spite of our failure to manifest it.

### *Practice:*

United Methodists are encouraged to continue participating in ecumenical services that include Holy Communion. Special care is to be given to the use of commonly approved texts or the development of liturgy that reflects the beliefs and practices of the different traditions. If bishops or superintendents are present, it is appropriate for them to be invited to preside.

Church members can practice hospitality by participating in each others' liturgies with attitudes of respect and openness to learning. United Methodists are encouraged to receive Communion in other churches when they are invited to do so.

Churches need to address, within official dialogues, the theological barriers to full Eucharistic sharing. Materials already available from the official dialogues shall be part of the study resources of the denomination.

United Methodists need to study and work to answer questions that are critical to ecumenical conversation and sensitive to ecumenical con-

This Holy Mystery

cerns—the presence of Christ ("real presence"), frequency of celebration, who presides at the Table, use of grape juice, and baptism in relation to Eucharist, among others.

⌁

### Principle:

United Methodists enter into the ecumenical conversation about Eucharist grounded in several historic sources of authority and relate most authentically to other Christian bodies as we remain faithful to these sources.

### Background:

Most prominent among United Methodism's sources of authority are the Scriptures of the Old and New Testaments; the hymns and writings of John and Charles Wesley (especially the Standard Sermons, the General Rules, and *Explanatory Notes Upon the New Testament*); the Constitution, Articles of Religion, Confession of Faith, and other doctrinal standards; the writings and traditions emerging from the evangelical experience, through the Wesleyan, Evangelical, and United Brethren movements; and current ecumenical developments and statements that have had United Methodist involvement, especially multilateral and bilateral agreements, some of which have been approved by the World Methodist Council and/or the General Conference.

"Our Doctrinal Heritage" points out some distinctive aspects of the United Methodist tradition:

> Although Wesley shared with many other Christians a belief in grace, justification, assurance, and sanctification, he combined them in a powerful manner to create distinctive emphases for living the full Christian life. The Evangelical United Brethren tradition, particularly as expressed by Phillip William Otterbein from a Reformed background, gave similar distinctive emphases.
>
> Grace pervades our understanding of Christian faith and life. By grace we mean the undeserved, unmerited, and loving action of God in human existence through the ever-present Holy Spirit. While the grace of God is undivided, it precedes salvation as "prevenient grace," continues in "justifying grace," and is brought to fruition in "sanctifying grace."
>
> (BOD; pages 45–46)

> These distinctive emphases of United Methodists provide the basis for "practical divinity," the experiential realization of the gospel of Jesus Christ in the lives of Christian people. These emphases have been preserved not so much through formal doctrinal declarations as through the vital movement of faith and practice as seen in converted lives and within the disciplined life of the Church.

Devising formal definitions of doctrine has been less pressing for United Methodists than summoning people to faith and nurturing them in the knowledge and love of God. The core of Wesleyan doctrine that informed our past rightly belongs to our common heritage as Christians and remains a prime component within our continuing theological task.

(*BOD*; pages 49–50)

The General Commission on Christian Unity and Interreligious Concerns spearheads the ecumenical work of the denomination by fulfilling its purpose: "To advocate and work toward the full reception of the gift of Christian unity in every aspect of the Church's life and to foster approaches to ministry and mission that more fully reflect the oneness of Christ's church in the human community" (*BOD*; ¶ 1902.1).

In "Resolution of Intent—With a View to Unity," the 2000 General Conference declared it "our official intent henceforth to interpret all our Articles, Confession, and other 'standards of doctrine' in consonance with our best ecumenical insights and judgment" (*BOR*; page 273).

### Practice:

Within all discussions of Holy Communion, United Methodism must remain firmly anchored in its traditional sources of authority. We recognize and respect authorities that other church traditions hold dear. United Methodists remain open to greater Christian unity through the work of the Holy Spirit in response to Jesus' prayer that "they may all be one" (John 17:21).

## Endnotes

1 From "A Service of Word and Table I," © 1972, 1980, 1985, 1989 The United Methodist Publishing House.
2 From Preface to *Hymns and Sacred Poems*.
3 From "The Baptismal Covenant I," © 1976, 1980, 1985, 1989, 1992 UMPH.
4 Both from "A Service of Word and Table I."
5 From "Baptism, Eucharist and Ministry," © 1982 WCC Publications, World Council of Churches, PO Box 2100, 1211 Geneva 2, Geneva, Switzerland; page 14.

# Wesleyan Way or Order of Salvation

In Wesleyan theology, salvation is a process, not an event; it is dynamic rather than static. We are to grow into the image of Christ over time but can also backslide in our spiritual journeys. The points listed below are, therefore, not to be understood as fixed, ordered steps, but as realities and experiences that are aspects of our being brought into saving relationship with God through Jesus Christ.

**Goodness of God's Creation**

**Sin**—human misuse of freedom of will

**God's Actions for Human Salvation**—the theme of the Bible: God must always take the initiative before we can respond.
    **Old Testament Covenant**—between God and the Hebrew/Israelite/Jewish people
    **New Testament Covenant**—between God and the Christian church through the work of Christ

**Christian Church**—the body of Christ; continues Christ's work of redeeming the world

God works in the church through **Means of Grace**—prayer, worship, Bible reading, fasting, Christian conferencing, for example

**Sacraments** are special means of grace—sign-acts of the church through which divine grace is conveyed to us
    **Baptism**—signals our initiation into the church; gives us our identity and mission
    **Holy Communion**—sustains and empowers us on our spiritual journeys

**Prevenient Grace**—God's gift to restore our ability to respond to God; conviction of sin

**Repentance and Faith**—our response of trusting in Christ

**Justification**—forgiveness that puts us into right relationship with God

**Regeneration**—born again; transformation; new spiritual life

**Assurance**—certainty that we are presently in saving relationship with God

**Falling From Grace/Faith**—sin reasserts itself; we make choices that retard our spiritual progress or even take us out of saving relationship with God

**Sanctification**—begins at regeneration, the lifelong process of growing in holiness

**Acts of Christian Discipleship**—working toward reconciliation and social justice

**Christian Perfection**—having advanced so far in the process of sanctification that we have no other motive except the love of God

**Glorification**—fullness of salvation beyond death

---

# Appendix

# The Duty of Constant Communion
## *John Wesley*

*THE following Discourse was written above five-and-fifty years ago, for the use of my pupils at Oxford. I have added very little, but retrenched much; as I then used more words than I do now. But, I thank God, I have not yet seen cause to alter my sentiments in any point which is therein delivered.*

*J. W.*
*1788*

"Do this in remembrance of me." (Luke xxii.19)

IT is no wonder that men who have no fear of God should never think of doing this. But it is strange that it should be neglected by any that do fear God, and desire to save their souls; and yet nothing is more common. One reason why many neglect it is, they are so much afraid of "eating and drinking unworthily," that they never think how much greater the danger is when they do not eat or drink it at all. That I may do what I can to bring these well-meaning men to a more just way of thinking, I shall,

I. Show that it is the duty of every Christian to receive the Lord's Supper as often as he can; and,

II. Answer some objections

I. I am to show that it is the duty of every Christian to receive the Lord's Supper as often as he can.

1. The First reason why it is the duty of every Christian so to do is, because it is a plain command of Christ. That this is his command, appears from the words of the text, "Do this in remembrance of me:" By which, as the Apostles were obliged to bless, break, and give the bread to all that joined with them in these holy things; so were all Christians obliged to receive those signs of Christ's body and blood. Here, therefore, the bread and wine are commanded to be received, in remembrance of his death, to the end of the world. Observe, too, that this command was given by our Lord when he was just laying down his life for our sakes. They are, therefore, as it were, his dying words to all his followers.

2. A Second reason why every Christian should do this as often as he can, is, because the benefits of doing it are so great to all that do it in obedience to him; viz., the forgiveness of our past sins, the present strengthening and refreshing of our souls. In this world we are never free from temptations. Whatever way of life we are in, whatever our condition be, whether we are sick or well, in trouble or at ease, the enemies of our souls are watching to lead us into sin. And too often they prevail over us. Now, when we are convinced of having sinned against God, what surer way have we of procuring pardon from him, than the "showing forth the Lord's death;" and beseeching him, for the sake of his Son's sufferings, to blot out all our sins?

3. The grace of God given herein confirms to us the pardon of our sins, and enables us to leave them. As our bodies are strengthened by bread and wine, so are our souls by these tokens of the body and the blood of Christ. This is the food of our souls: This gives strength to perform our duty, and leads us on to perfection. If, therefore, we have any regard for the plain command of Christ, if we desire the pardon of our sins, if we wish for strength to believe, to love and obey God, then we should neglect no opportunity of receiving the Lord's Supper; then we must never turn our backs on the feast which our Lord has prepared for us. We must neglect no occasion, which the good providence of God affords us, for this purpose. This is the true rule: So often are we to receive as God gives us opportunity. Whoever, therefore, does not receive, but goes from the holy table, when all things are prepared, either does not understand his duty, or does not care for the dying command of his Saviour, the forgiveness of his sins, the strengthening of his soul, and the refreshing it with the hope of glory.

4. Let every one therefore, who has either any desire to please God, or any love of his own soul, obey God, and consult the good of his own soul, by communicating every time he can; like the first Christians, with whom the Christian Sacrifice was a constant part of the Lord's day service. And for several centuries they received it almost every day: Four times a week always, and every Saint's day beside. Accordingly, those that joined in the prayers of the faithful never failed to partake of the blessed sacrament. What opinion they had of any who turned his back upon it, we may learn from that ancient canon:

"If any believer join in the prayers of the faithful, and go away without receiving the Lord's Supper, let him be excommunicated, as bringing confusion into the Church of God."

5. In order to understand the nature of the Lord's Supper, it would be useful carefully to read over those passages in the Gospel, and in the First Epistle to the Corinthians, which speak of the institution of it. Hence we learn that the design of this sacrament is, the continual remembrance of the death of Christ, by eating bread and drinking wine, which are the outward signs of the inward grace, the body and blood of Christ.

6. It is highly expedient for those who purpose to receive this, whenever their time will permit, to prepare themselves for this solemn ordinance by self-examination and prayer. But this is not absolutely necessary. And when we have not time for it, we should see that we have the habitual preparation which is absolutely necessary, and can never be dispensed with on any account or any occasion whatever. This is, First, a full purpose of heart to keep all the commandments of God; and, Secondly, a sincere desire to receive all his promises.

II. I am, in the Second place, to answer the common objections against constantly receiving the Lord's Supper.

1. I say constantly receiving; for as to the phrase of frequent communion, it is absurd to the last degree. If it means anything less than constant, it means more than can be proved to be the duty of any man. For if we are not obliged to communicate constantly, by what argument can it be proved that we are obliged to communicate frequently? yea, more than once a year, or once in seven years, or once before we die? Every argument brought for this, either proves that we ought to do it constantly, or proves nothing at all. Therefore, that indeterminate, unmeaning way of speaking ought to be laid aside by all men of understanding.

2. In order to prove that it is our duty to communicate constantly, we may observe that the holy communion is to be considered either, (1.) As a command of God; or, (2.) As a mercy to man.

First. As a command of God. God our Mediator and Governor, from whom we have received our life and all things, on whose will it depends whether we shall be perfectly happy or perfectly miserable from this moment to eternity, declares to us, that all who obey his commands shall be eternally happy; all who do not, shall be eternally miserable. Now, one of these commands is, "Do this in remembrance of me." I ask then, Why do you not do this, when you can do it if you will? When you have an opportunity before you, why do not you obey the command of God?

3. Perhaps you will say, "God does not command me to do this as often as I can:" That is, the words, "as often as you can," are not added in this particular place. What then? Are we not to obey every command of God as often as we can? Are not all the promises of God made to those, and those only, who "give all diligence;" that is, to those who do all they can to obey his commandments? Our power is the one rule of our duty. Whatever we can do, that we ought. With respect either to this or any other command, he that, when he may obey it if he will, does not, will have no place in the kingdom of heaven.

4. And this great truth, that we are obliged to keep every command as far as we can, is clearly proved from the absurdity of the contrary opinion; for were we to allow that we are not obliged to obey every commandment of God as often as we can, we have no argument left to prove that any man is

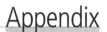

bound to obey any command at any time. For instance: Should I ask a man why he does not obey one of the plainest commands of God; why, for instance, he does not help his parents; he might answer, "I will not do it now; but I will at another time." When that time comes, put him in mind of God's command again; and he will say, "I will obey it some time or other." Nor is it possible ever to prove that he ought to do it now, unless by proving that he ought to do it as often as he can; and therefore he ought to do it now, because he can if he will.

5. Consider the Lord's Supper, Secondly, as a mercy from God to man. As God, whose mercy is over all his works, and particularly over the children of men, knew there was but one way for man to be happy like himself; namely, by being like him in holiness; as he knew we could do nothing towards this of ourselves, he has given us certain means of obtaining his help. One of these is the Lord's Supper, which, of his infinite mercy, he hath given for this very end; that through this means we may be assisted to attain those blessings which he hath prepared for us; that we may obtain holiness on earth, and everlasting glory in heaven.

I ask, then, Why do you not accept of his mercy as often as ever you can? God now offers you his blessing; — why do you refuse it? You have now an opportunity of receiving his mercy; — why do you not receive it? You are weak: — why do not you seize every opportunity of increasing your strength? In a word: Considering this as a command of God, he that does not communicate as often as he can has no piety; considering it as a mercy, he that does not communicate as often as he can has no wisdom.

6. These two considerations will yield a full answer to all the common objections which have been made against constant communion; indeed to all that ever were or can be made. In truth, nothing can be objected against it, but upon supposition that, this particular time, either the communion would be no mercy, or I am not commanded to receive it. Nay, should we grant it would be no mercy, that is not enough; for still the other reason would hold: Whether it does you any good or none, you are to obey the command of God.

7. However, let us see the particular excuses which men commonly make for not obeying it. The most common is, "I am unworthy; and 'he that eateth and drinketh unworthily, eateth and drinketh damnation to himself.' Therefore I dare not communicate, lest I should eat and drink my own damnation."

The case is this: God offers you one of the greatest mercies on this side heaven, and commands you to accept it. Why do not you accept this mercy, in obedience to his command? You say, "I am unworthy to receive it." And what then? You are unworthy to receive any mercy from God. But is that a reason for refusing all mercy? God offers you a pardon for all your sins. You are unworthy of it, it is sure, and he knows it; but since he is pleased to offer it nevertheless, will not you accept it? He offers to deliver your soul from death: You are unworthy to live; but will you therefore refuse life? He offers to endue your soul with new strength; because you are unworthy of its will you deny to take it? What can God himself do for us farther, if we refuse his mercy because we are unworthy of it?

8. But suppose this were no mercy to us; (to suppose which is indeed giving God the lie; saying, that is not good for man which he purposely ordered for his good;) still I ask, Why do not you obey God's command? He says, "Do this." Why do you not? You answer, "I am unworthy to do it." What! unworthy to obey God? unworthy to do what God bids you do? unworthy to obey God's command? What do you mean by this? that those who are unworthy to obey God ought not to obey him? Who told you so? If he were even "an angel from heaven, let him be accursed." If you think God himself has told you by St. Paul, let us hear his words. They are these: "He that eateth and drinketh unworthily, eateth and drinketh damnation to himself."

Why, this is quite another thing. Here is not a word said of being unworthy to eat and drink. Indeed he does speak of eating and drinking unworthily; but that is quite a different thing; so he has told us himself. In this very chapter we are told that by eating and drinking unworthily is meant, taking the holy Sacrament in such a rude and disorderly way, that one was "hungry, and another drunken." But what is that to you? Is there any danger of your doing so, — of your eating and drinking thus unworthily? However unworthy you are to communicate, there is no fear of your communicating thus. Therefore, whatever the punishment is, of doing it thus unworthily, it does not concern you. You have no more reason from this text to disobey God, than if there was no such text in the Bible. If you speak of "eating and drinking unworthily" in the sense St. Paul uses the words, you may as well say, "I dare not communicate, for fear the church should fall," as "for fear I should eat and drink unworthily."

9. If then you fear bringing damnation on yourself by this, you fear where no fear is. Fear it not, for eating and drinking unworthily; for that, in St. Paul's sense, ye cannot do. But I will tell you for what you shall fear damnation; — for not eating and drinking at all; for not obeying your Maker and Redeemer; for disobeying his plain command; for thus setting at nought both his mercy and authority. Fear ye this; for hear what his Apostle saith: "Whosoever shall keep the whole law, and yet offend in one point, is guilty of all." (James ii. 10.)

10. We see then how weak the objection is, "I dare not receive, because I am unworthy." Nor is it any stronger, though the reason why you think yourself unworthy is, that you have lately fallen into sin. It is true, our Church forbids those "who have done any grievous crime" to receive it without repentance. But all that follows from this is, that we should repent before we come; not that we should neglect to come at all.

To say, therefore, that "a man may turn his back upon the altar because he has lately fallen into sin, that he may impose this penance upon himself," is talking without any warrant from Scripture. For where does the Bible teach to atone for breaking one commandment of God by breaking another? What advice is this, — "Commit a new act of disobedience, and God will more easily forgive the past!"

11. Others there are who, to excuse their disobedience, plead that they are unworthy in another sense; that they "cannot

live up to it; they cannot pretend to lead so holy a life as constantly communicating would oblige them to do." Put this into plain words. I ask, Why do not you accept the mercy which God commands you to accept? You answer, "Because I cannot live up to the profession I must make when I receive it." Then it is plain you ought never to receive it at all. For it is no more lawful to promise once what you know you cannot perform, than to promise it a thousand times. You know too, that it is one and the same promise, whether you make it every year or every day. You promise to do just as much, whether you promise ever so often or ever so seldom.

If, therefore, you cannot live up to the profession they make who communicate once a week, neither can you come up to the profession you make who communicate once a year. But cannot you indeed? Then it had been good for you that you had never been born. For all that you profess at the Lord's table, you must both profess and keep, or you cannot be saved. For you profess nothing there but this, — that you will diligently keep his commandments. And cannot you keep up to this profession? Then you cannot enter into life.

12. Think then what you say, before you say you cannot live up to what is required of constant communicants. This is no more than is required of any communicants; yea, of every one that has a soul to be saved. So that to say, you cannot live up to this, is neither better nor worse than renouncing Christianity. It is, in effect, renouncing your baptism, wherein you solemnly promised to keep all his commandments. You now fly from that profession. You wilfully break one of his commandments, and, to excuse yourself, say, you cannot keep his commandments: Then you cannot expect to receive the promises, which are made only to those that keep them.

13. What has been said on this pretence against constant communion, is applicable to those who say the same thing in other words: "We dare not do it, because it requires so perfect an obedience afterwards as we cannot promise to perform." Nay, it requires neither more nor less perfect obedience than you promised in your baptism. You then

undertook to keep the commandments of God by his help; and you promise no more when you communicate.

14. A Second objection which is often made against constant communion, is, the having so much business as will not allow time for such a preparation as is necessary thereto. I answer, All the preparation that is absolutely necessary is contained in those words: "Repent you truly of your sins past; have faith in Christ our Saviour," (and observe, that word is not taken in its highest sense;) "amend your lives, and be in charity with all men; so shall ye be meet partakers of these holy mysteries." All who are thus prepared may draw near without fear, and receive the sacrament to their comfort. Now, what business can hinder you from being thus prepared? — from repenting of your past sins; from believing that Christ died to save sinners; from amending your lives, and being in charity with all men? No business can hinder you from this, unless it be such as hinders you from being in a state of salvation. If you resolve and design to follow Christ, you are fit to approach the Lord's table. If you do not design this, you are only fit for the table and company of devils.

15. No business, therefore, can hinder any man from having that preparation which alone is necessary, unless it be such as unprepares him for heaven, as puts him out of a state of salvation. Indeed every prudent man will, when he has time, examine himself before he receives the Lord's Supper, whether he repents him truly of his former sins; whether he believes the promises of God; whether he fully designs to walk in His ways, and be in charity with all men. In this, and in private prayer, he will doubtless spend all the time he conveniently can. But what is this to you who have not time? What excuse is this for not obeying God? He commands you to come, and prepare yourself by prayer, if you have time; if you have not, however, come. Make not reverence to God's command a pretence for breaking it. Do not rebel against him for fear of offending him. Whatever you do or leave undone besides, be sure to do what God bids you do. Examining yourself, and using private prayer, especially before the Lord's Supper, is good; but, behold! "to obey is better than" self-examination; "and to hearken," than the prayer of an angel.

16. A Third objection against constant communion is, that it abates our reverence for the sacrament. Suppose it did: What then? Will you thence conclude that you are not to receive it constantly? This does not follow. God commands you, "Do this." You may do it now, but will not, and, to excuse yourself, say, "If I do it so often, it will abate the reverence with which I do it now." Suppose it did; has God ever told you, that when the obeying his command abates your reverence to it, then you may disobey it? If he has, you are guiltless; if not, what you say is just nothing to the purpose. The law is clear. Either show that the Lawgiver makes this exception, or you are guilty before him.

17. Reverence for the sacrament may be of two sorts: Either such as is owing purely to the newness of the thing, such as men naturally have for anything they are not used to; or such as is owing to our faith, or to the love or fear of God. Now, the former of these is not properly a religious reverence, but purely natural. And this sort of reverence for the Lord's Supper, the constantly receiving of it must lessen. But it will not lessen the true religious reverence, but rather confirm and increase it.

18. A Fourth objection is, "I have communicated constantly so long, but I have not found the benefit I expected." This has been the case with many well meaning persons, and therefore deserves to be particularly considered. And consider this: First, whatever God commands us to do, we are to do because he commands, whether we feel any benefit thereby or no. Now, God commands, "Do this in remembrance of me." This, therefore, we are to do because he commands, whether we find present benefit thereby or not. But undoubtedly we shall find benefit sooner or later, though perhaps insensibly. We shall be insensibly strengthened, made more fit for the service of God, and more constant in it. At least, we are kept from falling back, and preserved from many sins and temptations: And surely this should be enough to make us receive this food as often as we can; though we do not presently feel the happy effects of it, as some have done, and we ourselves may when God sees best.

19. But suppose a man has often been at the sacrament, and yet received no benefit. Was it not his own fault? Either he was not rightly prepared, willing to obey all the commands and to receive all the promises of God, or he did not receive it aright, trusting in God. Only see that you are duly prepared for it, and the oftener you come to the Lord's table, the greater benefit you will find there.

20. A Fifth objection which some have made against constant communion is, that "the Church enjoins it only three times a year." The words of the Church are, "Note, that every parishioner shall communicate at the least three times in the year." To this I answer, First, What, if the Church had not enjoined it at all; is it not enough that God enjoins it? We obey the Church only for God's sake. And shall we not obey God himself? If, then, you receive three times a year because the Church commands it, receive every time you can because God commands it. Else your doing the one will be so far from excusing you for not doing the other, that your own practice will prove your folly and sin, and leave you without excuse.

But, Secondly, we cannot conclude from these words, that the Church excuses him who receives only thrice a year. The plain sense of them is, that he who does not receive thrice at least, shall be cast out of the Church: But they by no means excuse him who communicates no oftener. This never was the judgment of our Church: On the contrary, she takes all possible care that the sacrament be duly administered, wherever the Common Prayer is read, every Sunday and holiday in the year.

The Church gives a particular direction with regard to those that are in Holy Orders: "In all cathedral and collegiate Churches and Colleges, where there are many Priests and Deacons, they shall all receive the communion with the Priest, every Sunday at the least."

21. It has been shown, First, that if we consider the Lord's Supper as a command of Christ, no man can have any pretence to Christian piety, who does not receive it (not once a month, but) as often as he can. Secondly, that if we consider the institution of it, as a mercy to ourselves, no man who does not receive it as often as he can has any pretence to Christian prudence. Thirdly, that none of the objections usually made, can be any excuse for that man who does not, at every opportunity, obey this command and accept this mercy.

22. It has been particularly shown, First, that unworthiness is no excuse; because though in one sense we are all unworthy, yet none of us need be afraid of being unworthy in St. Paul's sense of "eating and drinking unworthily." Secondly, that the not having time enough for preparation can be no excuse; since the only preparation which is absolutely necessary, is that which no business can hinder; nor indeed anything on earth, unless so far as it hinders our being in a state of salvation. Thirdly, that its abating our reverence is no excuse; since he who gave the command, "Do this," nowhere adds, "unless it abates your reverence." Fourthly, that our not profiting by it is no excuse; since it is our own fault, in neglecting that necessary preparation which is in our own power. Lastly, that the judgment of our own Church is quite in favour of constant communion. If those who have hitherto neglected it on any of these pretences, will lay these things to heart, they will, by the grace of God, come to a better mind, and never more forsake their own mercies.

# Appendix

# A Service of Word and Table I

(Quoted from *The United Methodist Book of Worship*. Page references are to pages in the *Book of Worship*.)

*This service is found in UMH 6-11. A congregation may use this text for the entire service. It is desirable that during the course of the year the prayers in services of Word and Table be varied; see A Service of Word and Table II and III, the Great Thanksgivings (54-80), and resources for the Christian year (224-421). For further directions and options see 13-32.*

## ENTRANCE

GATHERING *See 16-17.*

GREETING *See 17-20.*

> The grace of the Lord Jesus Christ be with you.
> **And also with you.**
>
> The risen Christ is with us.
> **Praise the Lord!**

HYMN OF PRAISE * *See 17-20.*

OPENING PRAYER * *See 20-21.*

> *The following or a prayer of the day is offered:*
>
> **Almighty God,**
> **to you all hearts are open, all desires known,**
> **and from you no secrets are hidden.**
> **Cleanse the thoughts of our hearts**
> **by the inspiration of your Holy Spirit,**
> **that we may perfectly love you,**
> **and worthily magnify your holy name,**
> **through Christ our Lord. Amen.**

[ACTS OF PRAISE] *See 21-22.*

## PROCLAMATION AND RESPONSE

PRAYER FOR ILLUMINATION * *See 22.*

> **Lord, open our hearts and minds**
> **by the power of your Holy Spirit,**
> **that, as the Scriptures are read**
> **and your Word proclaimed,**
> **we may hear with joy what you say to us today.**
> **Amen.**

SCRIPTURE LESSON *See 22-23 and lectionary on 227-37.*

[PSALM] * *See 22-23 and lectionary on 227-37.*

[SCRIPTURE LESSON] *See 22-23 and lectionary on 227-37.*

HYMN OR SONG * *See 23.*

GOSPEL LESSON * *See 22-23 and lectionary on 227-37.*

SERMON *See 23.*

RESPONSE TO THE WORD *See 24.*

> **I believe in God, the Father Almighty,**
> **creator of heaven and earth.**
> **I believe in Jesus Christ, his only Son, our Lord,**
> **who was conceived by the Holy Spirit,**
> **born of the Virgin Mary,**
> **suffered under Pontius Pilate,**
> **was crucified, died, and was buried;**
> **he descended to the dead.**
> **On the third day he rose again;**
> **he ascended into heaven,**
> **is seated at the right hand of the Father,**
> **and will come again to judge the living**
> **and the dead.**

I believe in the Holy Spirit,
    the holy catholic* church,     *universal
    the communion of saints,
    the forgiveness of sins,
    the resurrection of the body,
    and the life everlasting. Amen.

## CONCERNS AND PRAYERS * *See 24-25.*

*Brief intercessions, petitions, and thanksgivings may be prayed by the leader or spontaneously by members of the congregation. To each of these, all may make a common response, such as:*
**Lord, hear our prayer** *or UMH 485, 487, 488, or 490.*

*Or a litany of intercession and petition may be prayed. See 495.*

*Or a pastoral prayer may be prayed. See 25.*

## INVITATION

*Pastor stands behind the Lord's table.*

Christ our Lord invites to his table all who love him,
    who earnestly repent of their sin
    and seek to live in peace with one another.
Therefore, let us confess our sin before God and one
    another.

## CONFESSION AND PARDON *See 20-21, 25-26.*

**Merciful God,**
    **we confess that we have not loved you with our**
        **whole heart.**
**We have failed to be an obedient church.**
**We have not done your will,**
    **we have broken your law,**
    **we have rebelled against your love,**
    **we have not loved our neighbors,**
    **and we have not heard the cry of the needy.**
**Forgive us, we pray.**
**Free us for joyful obedience,**
    **through Jesus Christ our Lord. Amen.**

*All pray in silence.*

*Leader to people:*

Hear the good news:
    Christ died for us while we were yet sinners;
    that proves God's love toward us.
In the name of Jesus Christ, you are forgiven!

*People to leader:*

**In the name of Jesus Christ, you are forgiven!**

*Leader and people:*

**Glory to God. Amen.**

## THE PEACE * *See 26.*

Let us offer one another signs of reconciliation and love.

*All, including the pastor, exchange signs and words of God's peace.*

## OFFERING *See 26-27.*

As forgiven and reconciled people,
    let us offer ourselves and our gifts to God.

*A hymn, psalm, or anthem may be sung as the offering is received.*

*The bread and wine are brought by representatives of the people to the Lord's table with the other gifts, or uncovered if already in place.*

*A hymn, doxology, or other response may be sung as the gifts are presented.*

*If a Great Thanksgiving other than that which follows here is to be used, the service proceeds with A Service of Word and Table III (40). Otherwise, the service continues as follows:*

### THANKSGIVING AND COMMUNION

## TAKING THE BREAD AND CUP *See 27-28*

*The pastor, standing if possible behind the Lord's table, facing the people from this time through Breaking the Bread, takes the bread and cup; and the bread and wine are prepared for the meal.*

## THE GREAT THANKSGIVING * *See 28.*

*One of the musical settings in UMH 17-25 may be used, the pastor using the following text:*

The Lord be with you.
**And also with you.**
Lift up your hearts. *The pastor may lift hands and keep them raised.*
**We lift them up to the Lord.**
Let us give thanks to the Lord our God.
**It is right to give our thanks and praise.**

It is right, and a good and joyful thing,
    always and everywhere to give thanks to you,
    Father Almighty, creator of heaven and earth.
You formed us in your image
    and breathed into us the breath of life.
When we turned away, and our love failed,
    your love remained steadfast.
You delivered us from captivity,
    made covenant to be our sovereign God,
    and spoke to us through the prophets.

And so,
    with your people on earth
    and all the company of heaven
    we praise your name and join their unending hymn:

*The pastor may lower hands.*

**Holy, holy, holy Lord, God of power and might,
heaven and earth are full of your glory.**
    **Hosanna in the highest.**
**Blessed is he who comes in the name of the Lord.**
    **Hosanna in the highest.**

*The pastor may raise hands.*

Holy are you, and blessed is your Son Jesus Christ.
Your Spirit anointed him
    to preach good news to the poor,
    to proclaim release to the captives
        and recovering of sight to the blind,
    to set at liberty those who are oppressed,

and to announce that the time had come
    when you would save your people.
He healed the sick, fed the hungry, and ate with sinners.
By the baptism of his suffering, death, and resurrection
    you gave birth to your Church,
    delivered us from slavery to sin and death,
    and made with us a new covenant
        by water and the Spirit.
When the Lord Jesus ascended,
    he promised to be with us always,
        in the power of your Word and Holy Spirit.

*The pastor may hold hands, palms down, over the bread, or touch the bread, or lift the bread.*

On the night in which he gave himself up for us,
    he took bread, gave thanks to you, broke the bread,
    gave it to his disciples, and said:
"Take, eat; this is my body which is given for you.
Do this in remembrance of me."

*The pastor may hold hands, palms down, over the cup, or touch the cup, or lift the cup.*

When the supper was over, he took the cup,
    gave thanks to you, gave it to his disciples, and said:
"Drink from this, all of you;
    this is my blood of the new covenant,
    poured out for you and for many
        for the forgiveness of sins.
Do this, as often as you drink it,
    in remembrance of me."

*The pastor may raise hands.*

And so,
in remembrance of these your mighty acts in
        Jesus Christ,
we offer ourselves in praise and thanksgiving
    as a holy and living sacrifice,
    in union with Christ's offering for us,
as we proclaim the mystery of faith.

**Christ has died; Christ is risen; Christ will
        come again.**

*The pastor may hold hands, palms down, over the bread and cup.*

Pour out your Holy Spirit on us gathered here,
    and on these gifts of bread and wine.
Make them be for us the body and blood of Christ,
that we may be for the world the body of Christ,
    redeemed by his blood.

*The pastor may raise hands.*

By your Spirit make us one with Christ,
    one with each other,
    and one in ministry to all the world,
until Christ comes in final victory
    and we feast at his heavenly banquet.

Through your Son Jesus Christ,
with the Holy Spirit in your holy Church,
all honor and glory is yours, almighty Father,
now and for ever. **Amen.**

## THE LORD'S PRAYER * *See 29.*

*The pastor's hands may be extended in open invitation.*

And now, with the confidence of children of God, let us pray:

*The pastor may raise hands.*

**Our Father in heaven,**
    **hallowed be your name,**
    **your kingdom come,**
    **your will be done,**
        **on earth as in heaven.**
**Give us today our daily bread.**
**Forgive us our sins**
    **as we forgive those who sin against us.**
**Save us from the time of trial,**
    **and deliver us from evil.**
**For the kingdom, the power, and the glory**
     **are yours**
     **now and for ever. Amen.**

## BREAKING THE BREAD *See 29.*

*The pastor, still standing behind the Lord's table facing the people, breaks the bread in silence, or while saying:*

Because there is one loaf,
we, who are many, are one body, for we all partake of
    the one loaf.
The bread which we break is a sharing in the body
    of Christ.

*The pastor lifts the cup in silence, or while saying:*

The cup over which we give thanks is a sharing in the
    blood of Christ.

## GIVING THE BREAD AND CUP *See 29-31.*

*The bread and wine are given to the people, with these or other words being exchanged:*

The body of Christ, given for you. **Amen.**
The blood of Christ, given for you. **Amen.**

*The congregation may sing hymns while the bread and cup are given. Many hymns, songs, and choruses in* UMH *in addition to 612-41 and others listed under Holy Communion (943) are effective in expressing the people's loving communion with God and with one another. The day or season of the Christian year and the people's knowledge and love of particular hymns are important considerations in the selection of appropriate hymns. It is particularly effective if the people can sing from memory.*

*When all have received, the Lord's table is put in order. See 30.*

*The following prayer is then offered by the pastor or by all:*

**Eternal God, we give you thanks for this holy mystery**
    **in which you have given yourself to us.**
**Grant that we may go into the world**
    **in the strength of your Spirit,**
    **to give ourselves for others,**
**in the name of Jesus Christ our Lord. Amen.**

SENDING FORTH

HYMN OR SONG * *See 30-31.*

DISMISSAL WITH BLESSING * *See 31-32.*

> Go forth in peace.
> The grace of the Lord Jesus Christ,
> and the love of God,
> and the communion of the Holy Spirit
> be with you all. **Amen.**

GOING FORTH * *See 32.*

"A Service of Word and Table I" © 1972 The Methodist Publishing House; © 1980, 1985, 1989, 1992 The United Methodist Publishing House. Used by permission.

# A Service of Word and Table V
# With Persons Who Are Sick or Homebound

(Quoted from *The United Methodist Book of Worship*. Page references are to pages in the *Book of Worship*.)

*Since the earliest Christian times, communion has been brought as an extension of the congregation's worship to sick or homebound persons unable to attend congregational worship.*

*The following service is very flexible, depending upon the circumstances of the pastoral visit. "The people" may be simply the pastor and one other person. The service may be very informal and conversational. There should be every possible sensitivity to the particular needs of the person(s) receiving communion.*

*Guidelines for abridging A Service of Word and Table IV for use with sick or homebound persons are found on 41.*

*The pastor, or laypersons at the direction of the pastor, may distribute the consecrated bread and cup to sick or homebound persons as soon as feasible following a service of Word and Table as an extension of that service. When this service is used as a distribution of the consecrated bread and cup, the Great Thanksgiving is omitted, but thanks should be given after the bread and cup are received.*

*There should be whatever participation is feasible by those receiving communion. Sometimes this may simply be gestures and expression. Familiar acts of worship that persons may know by memory—the Lord's Prayer, the Apostles' Creed, or the Twenty-third Psalm, for instance—may be used. Sometimes it is possible to sing one or more hymns.*

*Those distributing communion should also be sensitive to the power of acts such as calling the person by name, touching the person, encouraging the remembrance of significant experiences, and allowing sick or homebound persons to minister to the visitors.*

*The people come together and exchange greetings in the Lord's name.*

*Scriptures are read and interpreted, and prayer and praise are offered.*

## INVITATION

Christ our Lord invites to his table
    all who love him and seek to grow into his likeness.
Let us draw near with faith, make our humble
    confession,
    and prepare to receive this Holy Sacrament.

## CONFESSION AND PARDON

**We do not presume to come to this your table,
    merciful Lord,
      trusting in our own goodness, but in your
      unfailing mercies.
We are not worthy that you should receive us,
but give your word and we shall be healed,
through Jesus Christ our Lord. Amen.**

Hear the good news:
    Christ died for us while we were yet sinners;
    that is proof of God's love toward us.
In the name of Jesus Christ, you are forgiven!

## THE PEACE

*Signs and words of God's peace are exchanged.*

## TAKING THE BREAD AND CUP

*The bread and wine are prepared for the meal.*

## THE GREAT THANKSGIVING *See 28, 80.*

*The pastor prays as follows if the bread and cup are to be consecrated. If they have already been consecrated, this prayer is omitted.*

*If a layperson is distributing the consecrated bread and cup, this prayer is omitted.*

Lift up your heart(s) and give thanks to the Lord
    our God.

Father Almighty, Creator of heaven and earth,
    you made us in your image, to love and to be loved.
When we turned away, and our love failed, your love
    remained steadfast.
By the suffering, death, and resurrection of your only
    Son Jesus Christ
      you delivered us from slavery to sin and death
      and made with us a new covenant by water and
      the Spirit.

On the night in which Jesus gave himself up for us he
    took bread,
      gave thanks to you, broke the bread, gave it to his
      disciples, and said:
"Take, eat; this is my body which is given for you.
Do this in remembrance of me."

When the supper was over he took the cup,
    gave thanks to you, gave it to his disciples, and said:
"Drink from this, all of you; this is my blood of the new
    covenant,
      poured out for you and for many for the forgiveness
      of sins.
Do this, as often as you drink it, in remembrance of me."

And so, in remembrance of these your mighty acts in
    Jesus Christ,
we offer ourselves in praise and thanksgiving
    as a holy and living sacrifice, in union with Christ's
    offering for us.
Pour out your Holy Spirit on us, and on these gifts of
    bread and wine.
Make them be for us the body and blood of Christ,
    that we may be for the world the body of Christ,
    redeemed by his blood.

By your Spirit make us one with Christ, one with
    each other,
    and one in ministry to all the world,

until Christ comes in final victory, and we feast at his
    heavenly banquet.
Through your Son Jesus Christ, with the Holy Spirit in
    your holy Church,
all honor and glory is yours, almighty Father, now and
    for ever. Amen.

## THE LORD'S PRAYER

## BREAKING THE BREAK

*In silence or with appropriate words.*

## GIVING THE BREAD AND CUP

*With these or other words being exchanged:*

*Name*, the body of Christ, given for you. **Amen.**
*Name*, the blood of Christ, given for you. **Amen.**

*When all have received, the Lord's table is put in order.*

*Thanks may be given after communion. A hymn, song, or chorus may be sung. If the consecrated bread and cup have been given and there has been no Great Thanksgiving, the following prayer is suggested after Communion:*

Most bountiful God, we give you thanks for the world
    you have created,
      for the gift of life, and for giving yourself to us in
      Jesus Christ,
      whose holy life, suffering and death, and glorious resurrection
      have delivered us from slavery to sin and death.
We thank you that in the power of your Holy Spirit
    you have fed us in this Sacrament, united us with
      Christ,
    and given us a foretaste of your heavenly banquet.
We are your children, and yours is the glory, now and
    for ever;
through Jesus Christ our Lord. **Amen.**

BLESSING

> The grace of the Lord Jesus Christ,
> and the love of God,
> and the communion of the Holy Spirit
> be with you [all]. **Amen.**